BROTHER BRIGHAM'S WAY TO WEALTH

Brother Brigham's
WAY TO WEALTH

*How to Acquire and Use Worldly Goods
in the Lord's Service*

*A Compilation of Counsel from
President Brigham Young*

TEMPLE HILL BOOKS

ISBN 978-1-4341-0427-4

Published by Temple Hill Books, an imprint of The Editorium

Temple Hill Books™, the Temple Hill Books logo, and The Editorium™ are trademarks of The Editorium, LLC

The Editorium, LLC
West Jordan, UT 84081-6132
templehillbooks.com
templehillbooks@editorium.com

Contents

PREFACE

President Brigham Young understood wealth—how to acquire it and how to use it in the Lord's service. And he spent much of his time passing that understanding on to the Saints he so ably governed. His aim was not just to preserve life or to promote comfort and convenience but to build the kingdom of God and establish Zion:

> Let us train our minds until we delight in that which is good, lovely and holy, seeking continually after that intelligence which will enable us effectually to build up Zion, which consists in building houses, tabernacles, temples, streets, and every convenience and necessity to embellish and beautify, seeking to do the will of the Lord all the days of our lives, improving our minds in all scientific and mechanical knowledge, seeking diligently to understand the great design and plan of all created things, that we may know what to do with our lives and how to improve upon the facilities placed within our reach. (*Discourses of Brigham Young*, 247.)

Those who followed his counsel were able to establish cities and settlements, to provide for themselves and their neighbors, turning dry deserts into fields and farmlands, with orchards and gardens to please the eye and gladden the heart.

In our modern world, some of Brother Brigham's counsel may seem outdated. Few of us now have the ability to keep a cow or spin wool into yarn. But if we can understand and apply the principles *behind* his teaching, we can do much to improve our lives and enhance our self-reliance. The purpose of this book is to help us do that.

> If I improve upon what the Lord has given me, and continue to improve, I shall become like those who have gone before me; I shall be exalted in the celestial kingdom, and be filled to overflowing with all the power I can wield; and all the keys of knowledge I can manage will be committed unto me. (*Discourses of Brigham Young,* 460.)

❖ *Chapter the First* ❖

ACQUIRING WEALTH

Self-Reliance

Instead of searching after what the Lord is going to do for us, let us inquire what we can do for ourselves. (*Journal of Discourses* 9:172.)

If we do not take care of ourselves, we shall have a very poor chance to be taken care of. (*Journal of Discourses* 12:204.)

A great many think that the Kingdom of God is going to bless them and exalt them, without any efforts on their part. This is not so. Every man and woman is expected to aid the work with all the ability God has given them. (*Discourses of Brigham Young,* 444.)

Who supported my family? God and I. Who found me clothing? The Lord and myself. (*Journal of Discourses* 7:229.)

All persons that will not try to take care of themselves, will see a day of sorrow, and will regret the waste of time misspent in this life. (*Journal of Discourses* 4:318.)

If nobody will speak for us, let us speak for ourselves; if no person else will do anything for us, let us do something for ourselves. This is right; it is politically right, religiously right, nationally right, socially and morally right, and it is right in every sense of the word for us to sustain ourselves. (*Discourses of Brigham Young,* 358.)

Brethren, learn. You have learned a good deal, it is true; but learn more; learn to sustain yourselves; lay up grain and flour, and save it against a day of scarcity. Sisters, do not ask your husbands to sell the last bushel of grain you have to buy something for you out of the stores, but aid your husbands in storing it up against a day of want, and always have a year's, or two, provision on hand. (*Journal of Discourses* 12:204.)

If we could only learn enough to be self-preserving and self-sustaining, we should then have learned what the Gods have learned before us, and what we must eventually learn before we can be exalted. (*Discourses of Brigham Young,* 255.)

We are prepared for some things, and we receive just as fast as we prepare ourselves. (*Discourses of Brigham Young,* 95.)

While we have a rich soil in this valley, and seed to put in the ground, we need not ask God to feed us, nor follow us round with a loaf of bread begging of us to eat it. He will not do it, neither would I, were I the Lord. We can feed ourselves here; and if we are ever placed in circumstances where we cannot, it will then be time enough for the Lord to work a miracle to sustain us. (*Journal of Discourses* 1:108.)

Who are deserving of praise? The persons who take care of themselves or the ones who always trust in the great mercies of the Lord to take care of them? It is just as consistent to expect that the Lord will supply us with fruit when we do not plant the trees; or that when we do not plow and sow and are saved the labor of harvesting, we should cry to the Lord to save us from want, as to ask him to save us from the consequences of our own folly, disobedience and waste. (*Journal of Discourses* 12:243–244.)

We have men who quarry rock out of the mountains; and we would say to those men, can you go and quarry rock without the suitable instruments? Says one, I must have so many picks and wedges, and I must have so many drills of different sizes, and so many sledges and hammers.

Another man says, I am going to make the tools; I have the ability, and I will make the instruments from the ore in the mountain. You remember what Nephi did. When he came to the sea, and prepared to build his barge, the Lord showed him the ore, and Nephi made the tools with which he formed his barge. He did not have to go back to Jerusalem to get tools. I would like to see a little more of that skill displayed here than I do at the present time. I am using this comparison to show that we, in our poverty, have this work to do. (*Journal of Discourses* 8:354.)

We want you henceforth to be a self-sustaining people. Hear it, O Israel! hear it, neighbors, friends and enemies, this is what the Lord requires of this people. (*Journal of Discourses* 12:285.)

What hinders you from raising something to feed a cow? Nothing. Who hinders you from planting your garden with corn, and having the suckers and the fodder? Who hinders you from raising carrots, parsnips, etc., to feed a cow with through the winter? This you can do on a little more than a quarter of an acre, but will you do it? (*Journal of Discourses* 4:317.)

Go into the garden and raise the salad and numerous other articles within your judgment and strength. Who hindered you from making a little vinegar last year? People are frequently running round and asking, Where can I buy some vinegar? When I was keeping a house, if my neighbors had a million hogsheads of vinegar, I had no need to buy a spoonful of it, for I would make a plenty for my own use, and would have eggs, butter, and pork, of my own production, and manage to secure beef, and salt it away nicely, and we had all the essentials for comfortable diet. (*Journal of Discourses* 4:318.)

Ye Latter-day Saints, learn to sustain yourselves, produce everything you need to eat, drink or wear; and if you cannot obtain all you wish for today, learn to do without that which you cannot purchase and pay for; and bring your minds into subjection that you must and will live within your means. (*Journal of Discourses* 12:231.)

You have a living off an acre and a quarter of land. Such a little farm well tilled and well managed, and the products of it economically applied, will do wonders towards keeping and educating a small family. Let the little children do their part, when they are not engaged in their studies, in knitting their stockings and mittens, braiding straw for their hats, or spinning yarn for their frocks and underclothing. If this people would strictly observe these simple principles of economy, they would soon become so rich that they would not have room sufficient to hold their abundance; their storehouses would run over with fulness. (*Journal of Discourses* 11:142.)

My faith does not lead me to think the Lord will provide us with roast pigs, bread already buttered, etc.; he will give us the ability to raise the grain, to obtain the fruits of the earth, to make habitations, to procure a few boards to make a box, and when harvest comes, giving us the grain, it is for us to preserve it—to save the wheat until we have one, two, five, or seven years' provisions on hand, until there is enough of the staff of life saved by the people to [provide] bread [for] themselves and those who will come here seeking for safety. (*Journal of Discourses* 10.293.)

It is a shame that men and women do not pay more attention to the principles of economy in living. They want to have money to go to market and buy everything ready made. They want to have somebody feed them. I have thought, many times, that some persons would not be satisfied, unless we baked plum puddings, and roasted beef for them, and then fed them while they were lounging in big easy chairs; and still perhaps they would think that they were ill treated, if we did not chew the meat for them. (*Journal of Discourses,* 4:315.)

If you cannot provide for your natural lives, how can you expect to have wisdom to obtain eternal lives? God has given you your existence—your body and spirit, and has blest you with ability, and thereby laid the foundation of all knowledge, wisdom, and understanding, and all glory and eternal lives. If you have not attained ability to provide for your natural wants, . . . what have you to do with heavenly things? (*Discourses of Brigham Young,* 13.)

I do not expect to see the day when I am perfectly independent, until I am crowned in the celestial kingdom of my Father, and made as independent as my Father in Heaven. I have not yet received my inheritance as my own, and I expect to be dependent until I do, for all that I have is lent to me. (*Journal of Discourses* 3:245.)

The Nature of Wealth

Earthly riches are concealed in the elements God has given to man, and the essence of wealth is power to organize from these elements every comfort and convenience of life for our sustenance here, and for eternal existence hereafter. The possession of all the gold and silver in the world would not satisfy the cravings of the immortal soul of man. The gift of the Holy Spirit of the Lord alone can produce a good, wholesome, contented mind. Instead of looking for gold and silver, look to the heavens and try to learn wisdom until you can organize the native elements for your benefit; then, and not until then, will you begin to possess the true riches. (*Journal of Discourses* 10:35.)

All the capital there is upon the earth is the bone and sinew of workingmen and women. Were it not for that, the gold and the silver and precious stones would remain in the mountains, upon the plains and in the valleys, and never would be gathered or brought into use. The timber would continue to grow, but none of it would be brought into service, and the earth would remain as it is; but it is the activity and labor of the inhabitants of the earth that bring forth the wealth. Labor builds our meetinghouses, temples, courthouses, fine halls for music and fine schoolhouses; it is labor that teaches our children, and makes them acquainted with the various branches of education, that makes them proficient in their own language and in other languages, and in every branch of knowledge understood by the children of men; and all this enhances the wealth and glory and the comfort of any people on the earth. (*Journal of Discourses* 16:66.)

Beautify your gardens, your houses, your farms; beautify the city. This will make us happy, and produce plenty. The earth is a good earth, the elements are good if we will use them for our own benefit, in truth and righteousness. Then let us be content, and go to with our mights to make ourselves healthy, wealthy, and beautiful, and preserve ourselves in the best possible manner, and live just as long as we can, and do all the good we can. (*Journal of Discourses* 15:20.)

Cultivate the earth and cultivate your minds. (*Journal of Discourses* 8:83.)

With regard to this railroad; when it is through, even in ordinary times it opens to us the market, and we are at the door of New York, right at the threshold of the emporium of the United States. We can send our butter, eggs, cheese, and fruits and receive in return oysters, clams, cod fish, mackerel, oranges, and lemons. Let me say more to you—do up your peaches in the best style, for they will want them. (*Journal of Discourses* 12:54.)

Daily toil, however humble it may be, is our daily duty, and by doing it well, we make it a part of our daily worship. (*Letters of Brigham Young to His Sons,* 191.)

Every improvement that we make not only adds to our comfort but to our wealth. (*Journal of Discourses* 16:64.)

Every man and woman that has talent and hides it will be called a slothful servant. Improve day by day upon the capital you have. In proportion as we are capacitated to receive, so it is our duty to do. (*Discourses of Brigham Young,* 248.)

It is our privilege and our duty to search all things upon the face of the earth, and learn what there is for man to enjoy, what God has ordained for the benefit and happiness of mankind, and then make use of it without sinning against him. (*Discourses of Brigham Young,* 254.)

It is the activity and labor of the inhabitants of the earth that bring forth the wealth. Labor builds our meeting houses, temples, court houses, fine halls for music and fine school houses; it is labor that teaches our children, and makes them acquainted with the various branches of education, that makes them proficient in their own language and in other languages, and in every branch of knowledge understood by the children of men; and all this enhances the wealth and the glory and the comfort of any people on the earth. (*Journal of Discourses* 16:66.)

I say to my brethren and sisters, come let us learn how to gather around us from the elements an abundance of every comfort of life, and convert them to our wants and happiness. Let us not remain ignorant, with the ignorant, but let us show the ignorant how to be wise. (*Journal of Discourses* 10:6.)

Let groves of olive trees be planted, and vineyards of the most approved varieties of grapes, and let sweet potatoes be raised in abundance, and all trees and roots that bear fruit in the ground and above the ground that can be used as food for man and beast, that plenty may flow in the land like a river, and contentment be enthroned in every household, while industry, frugality, and peace prevail everywhere. (*Journal of Discourses* 10:227.)

I want them to save their wool and to keep it in this Territory. If we have not factories sufficient to work up all the wool that grows in this Territory, and in these mountains, we will send and get more machinery, and build more factories, and work up the wool for the people. (*Journal of Discourses* 15:159.)

Go and build a tannery, that the hides that come off our beef cattle, can be made into leather. (*Journal of Discourses* 19:73.)

By-and-by some man will come along, not worth fifty dollars, and take the feldspar, which enters so largely into our granite rock, and make the best of chinaware. (*Journal of Discourses* 9:31.)

We want glass. Some man will come along, by-and-by, and take the quartz rock, rig up a little furnace and make glass. (*Journal of Discourses* 9:31.)

Go to and raise silk. You can do it, and those who cannot set themselves to work we will set them to work gathering straw, and making straw hats and straw bonnets; we will set others to gathering willow, and others to making baskets; we will set others to gathering flags and rushes, and to making mats, and bottoming chairs and making carpets. (*Journal of Discourses* 12:202.)

I pray the Lord to hedge up the way and shut down the gate so that we may be compelled to depend upon our own manufacturing for the comforts of life. (*Journal of Discourses* 7:67.)

The elements with which we are surrounded are as eternal as we are, and are loaded with supplies of every kind for the comfort and happiness of the human race. (*Discourses of Brigham Young,* 48.)

The elements are to be brought into shape and operation for the benefit, happiness, beauty, excellency, glory, and exaltation of the children of men that dwell upon the earth. (*Journal of Discourses* 9:242.)

God has given the children of men dominion over the earth and over all things that pertain to it and has commanded them to subdue it, and sanctify themselves before him, and also sanctify and beautify the earth by their industry and by their wisdom and skill which cometh from God. (*Journal of Discourses,* 10:25.)

True wealth consists in the skill to produce conveniences and comforts from the elements. All the power and dignity that wealth can bestow is a mere shadow, the substance is found in the bone and sinew of the toiling millions. Well directed labor is the true power that supplies our wants. It gives regal grandeur to potentates, education and supplies to religious and political ministers, and supplies the wants of the thousands of millions of earth's sons and daughters. (*Journal of Discourses* 10:189.)

The riches of a kingdom or nation do not consist so much in the fulness of its treasury as in the fertility of its soil and the industry of its people. (*Journal of Discourses* 10:266.)

If the Lord had a people on the earth that he had perfect confidence in, there is not a blessing in the eternities of our God that they could bear in the flesh, that he would not pour out upon them. Tongue cannot tell the blessings the Lord has for a people who have proved themselves before him. (*Discourses of Brigham Young,* 455.)

If the Latter-day Saints will walk up to their privileges and exercise faith in the name of Jesus Christ and live in the enjoyment of the fulness of the Holy Ghost constantly day by day, there is nothing on the face of the earth that they could ask for that would not be given to them. The Lord is waiting to be very gracious unto this people and to pour out upon them riches, honor, glory, and power, even that they may possess all things. (*Journal of Discourses,* 11:114.)

It matters little, though we have many times left our houses and other possessions, having been driven from them by our enemies; for the earth is the Lord's and the fulness thereof; the gold and silver they are taking from the earth are all in his hands to dispose of at his pleasure. He sets up kingdoms and casts them down at his pleasure. The fulness of the earth is in his hands, but it cannot be enjoyed, in the full sense of the term, without enjoying it in connection with his Kingdom. (*Journal of Discourses* 8:161–162.)

If you had the spirit of your calling, you would be anxious to build the best gardens, fields, and vineyards, though you knew that you would not enjoy them one day after they were completed. (*Journal of Discourses* 8:295.)

This world is before us. The gold, silver and precious stones are in the mountains, in the rivers, in the plains, in the sands and in the waters, they all belong to this world, and you and I belong to this world. Is there enough to make each of us a finger ring? Certainly there is. Is there enough to make us a breast pin? Certainly there is. Is there enough to make jewelry for the ladies to set their diamonds and precious stones in? Certainly there is. Is there enough to make the silver plate, the spoons, platters, plates and knives and forks? There is. There is plenty of it in the earth for all these purposes.

Then what on earth are you and I quarreling about it for? Go to work systematically and take it from the mountains, and put it to the use that we want it, without contending against each other, and filching the pockets of each other. The world is full of it. If it goes from my pocket it is still in the world, it still belongs to this little ball, this little speck in God's creation, so small that from the sun I expect you would have to have a telescope that would magnify it many times to see it; and from any of the fixed stars I do not expect that it has ever been seen, only by the celestials— mortals could not see this earth at that distance. And here people are contending, quarreling, seeking how to get the advantage of each other, and how to get all the wealth there is in the world; wanting to rule nations, wanting to be president, king or ruler.

What would they do if they were? Most of them would make everybody around them miserable, that is what they would do. There are very few men on the earth who try to make people happy. Occasionally there have been emperors and monarchs who have made their people happy but they have been very rare.

But suppose we go to work to gather up all that there is in the bosom and upon the surface of our mother earth and bring it into use, is there any lack? There is not, there is enough for all. Then do look at these things as they are, Latter-day Saints, and you who are not Latter-day Saints, look at things as they are. And I do hope and pray for your sakes, outsiders, and for the sakes of those who profess to be Latter-day Saints, that we shall have good peace for a time here, so that we can build our furnaces, open our mines, make our railroads, till the soil, follow our mercantile business uninterrupted; that we may attend to the business of beautifying the earth. (*Journal of Discourses* 15:19.)

To possess this world's goods is not in reality wealth, it is not riches, it is nothing more nor less than that which is common to all men, to the just and the unjust, to the Saint and to the sinner. The sun rises upon the evil and the good; the Lord sends his rain upon the just and upon the unjust; this is manifest before our eyes, and in our daily experience. Old King Solomon, the wise man, says, the race is not to the swift, nor the battle to the strong, neither riches to men of wisdom. The truth of this saying comes within our daily observation. Those whom we consider swift are not always the ones that gain the mastery in the race, but those who are considered not so fleet, or not fleet at all, often gain the prize. It is, I may say, the unseen hand of Providence, that overruling power that controls the destinies of men and nations, that so ordains these things. The weak, trembling, and feeble, are the ones frequently who gain the battle; and the ignorant, foolish, and unwise will blunder into wealth. This is all before us, it is the common lot of man; in short, I may say, it is the philosophical providence of a philosophical world. (*Journal of Discourses* 1:267.)

There is no such thing as a man being truly rich until he has power over death, hell, the grave, and him that hath the power of death, which is the Devil. For what are the riches, the wealth possessed by the inhabitants of the earth? Why, they are a phantom, a mere shadow, a bubble on the wave, that bursts with the least breath of air. Suppose I possessed millions on millions of wealth of every description I could think of or ask for, and I took a sudden pain in my head, which threw me entirely out of my mind, and baffled the skill of the most eminent physicians, what good would that money do me, in the absence of the power to say to the pain, Depart? But suppose I possessed power to say to the pain, Go thou to the land from whence thou comest; and say, Come, health, and give strength to my body; and when I want death, to say, Come you, for I have claim upon you, a right, a warranty deed, for this body must be dissolved; says death, I want it, to prey upon; but again I can say to death, Depart from me, thou canst not touch me; would I not be rich indeed? How is it now? Let the slightest accident come upon one of the human family, and they are no more. Do we then possess true riches in this state? We do not. (*Journal of Discourses* 1:271.)

No person on the earth can truly call anything his own, and never will until he has passed the ordeals we are all now passing, and has received his body again in a glorious resurrection, to be crowned by him who will be ordained and set apart to set a crown upon our heads. Then will be given to us that which we now only seem to own, and we will be forever one with the Father and the Son, and not until then. (*Journal of Discourses* 9:106.)

I wish the people to understand that they have no interest apart from the Lord our God. The moment you have a divided interest, that moment you sever yourselves from eternal principles. (*Journal of Discourses* 4:31.)

To me it is the Kingdom of God or nothing upon the earth. Without it I would not give a farthing for the wealth, glory, prestige and power of all the world combined; for like the dew upon the grass, it passeth away and is forgotten, and like the flower of the grass it withereth, and is not. Death levels the most powerful monarch with the poorest starving mendicant; and both must stand before the judgment seat of Christ to answer for the deeds done in the body. (*Discourses of Brigham Young*, 444–45.)

How contracted in mind and short-sighted we must be to permit the perishable things of this world to swerve us in the least degree from our fidelity to the truth. It shows that we lack knowledge which we should possess. (*Discourses of Brigham Young*, 231.)

Unless God blesses our exertions we shall have nothing. It is the Lord that gives the increase. (*Discourses of Brigham Young*, 22.)

We are nothing, only what the Lord makes us. (*Discourses of Brigham Young*, 22.)

Industry

When man is industrious and righteous, then is he happy. (*Discourses of Brigham Young*, 235.)

Is not the upbuilding of the Kingdom of God on earth a temporal labor all the time? It will be built up by physical force and means, by manual labor more than by any particular mental effort of the mind. (*Journal of Discourses* 3:122.)

It is our duty to be active and diligent in doing everything we can to sustain ourselves, to build up His Kingdom, to defend ourselves against our enemies, to lay our plans wisely, and to prosecute every method that can be devised to establish the Kingdom of God on the earth, and to sanctify and prepare ourselves to dwell in His presence. Yet, after all this, if the Lord should not help—if he should not lend his aid to our endeavors, all our labors will prove in vain. (*Journal of Discourses* 2:279–280.)

It is my mind that those who do nothing but sit in rocking-chairs can live on potatoes and buttermilk, while those who do the labour should have both the substantial food and the luxuries. My friends know that this is my mind all the time. (*Journal of Discourses* 8:201.)

Do you want wealth? If you do, do not be in a hurry. Do you want the riches pertaining to this world? Yes, we acknowledge we do. Then, be calm, contented, composed; keep your pulses correct, do not let them get up to a hundred and twenty, but keep them as high as you can ranging from seventy to seventy-six; and when there is an appointment for a meeting be sure to attend that meeting. If there is to be a two-days' meeting, come to it; spend the time here and learn what is going on. Watch closely, hear every word that is spoken, let every heart be lifted to God for wisdom, and know and understand every word of prophecy, every revelation that may be given, every counsel that may be presented to the people, that you may be able to weigh, measure, comprehend and decide between that which is of God and that which is not of God. Refuse the evil, learn wisdom, and grow in grace and in the knowledge of the truth. (*Journal of Discourses* 15:35.)

Efforts to accumulate property in the correct channel are far from being an injury to any community, on the contrary they are highly beneficial, provided individuals, with all that they have, always hold themselves in readiness to advance the interests of the Kingdom of God on the earth. Let every man and woman be industrious, prudent, and economical in their acts and feelings, and while gathering to themselves, let each one strive to identify his or her interests with the interests of this community, with those of their neighbor and neighborhood, let them seek their happiness and welfare in that of all, and we will be blessed and prospered. (*Journal of Discourses* 3:330.)

I can witness one fact, and so can others, that by paying attention to the building up of the Kingdom of God alone we have got rich in the things of this world; and if any man can tell how we can get rich in any other way, he can do more than I can. We leave our business and our families and go out to preach the peaceable things of the Kingdom, and pay attention to that, never thinking of our business or our families, except when we ask the Lord to bless our families in common with all the families of the Saints everywhere. (*Journal of Discourses* 11:116.)

I feel to urge these things upon the people that they may save themselves, that they may be industrious, and go to with a ready heart and willing mind, with all their might, to do the things that are necessary to be done. (*Journal of Discourses* 3:339.)

I intend to plant and sow, not only in the month of May, but in the month of June, and in the month of July, and I will continue my labors to raise what is necessary to sustain life, as long as the season lasts. (*Journal of Discourses* 2:280.)

My policy is to keep every man, woman, and child busily employed, that they may have no idle time for hatching mischief in the night, and for making plans to accomplish their own ruin. (*Journal of Discourses* 2:144.)

My policy is to keep everybody busy in building up this kingdom; in building houses; in breaking up land; in setting out fruit and ornamental trees; in laying out fine gardens, pleasant walks, and beautiful groves; and in building academies, and other places of learning. (*Journal of Discourses* 2:145.)

Let the Latter-day Saints neglect their labor, and they will soon find that they are declining in their feelings, tastes and judgment for improving the elements of the earth; hence we say, improve, be industrious, prudent, faithful, make good farms, gardens and orchards, good public and private buildings, have the best schools, &c. The world give us the credit of being the most industrious people on the face of the earth. (*Journal of Discourses* 16:66.)

Improvement belongs to the spirit and plan of the heavens. (*Journal of Discourses* 16:65.)

Learn to be good for something. (*Discourses of Brigham Young,* 255.)

Let the people build good houses, plant good vineyards and orchards, make good roads, build beautiful cities in which may be found magnificent edifices for the convenience of the public, handsome streets skirted with shade trees, fountains of water, crystal streams, and every tree, shrub and flower that will flourish in this climate, to make our mountain home a paradise and our hearts wells of gratitude to the God of Joseph, enjoying it all with thankful hearts, saying constantly, not mine but thy will be done, O Father. (*Journal of Discourses* 10:3.)

Let us develop the variety within us, and show to the world that we have talent and taste, and prove to the heavens that our minds are set on beauty and true excellence, so that we can become worthy to enjoy the society of angels, and raise ourselves above the level of the wicked world and begin to increase in faith, and the power that God has given us, and to show to the world an example worthy of imitation. (*Discourses of Brigham Young,* 424.)

Make good houses; learn how to build; become good mechanics and business men, that you may know how to build a house, a barn, or a storehouse, how to make a farm, and how to raise stock, and take every care of it by providing proper shelter and every suitable convenience for keeping it through the winter; and prove yourselves worthy of the greater riches that will be committed to you than this valley and what it can produce. (*Journal of Discourses* 8:289.)

My policy is to get rich; I am a miser in eternal things. Do I want to become rich in the things of this earth? Yes, if the

Lord wishes me to have such riches, and I can use them to good advantage. (*Journal of Discourses* 2:144.)

Shall I give you my ideas in brief with regard to business and business transactions? Here for instance, a merchant comes to our neighborhood with a stock of goods; he sells them at from two to ten hundred per cent above what they cost. As a matter of course he soon becomes wealthy, and after a time he will be called a millionaire, when perhaps he was not worth a dollar when he commenced to trade. You will hear many say of such person, what a nice man he is, and what a great financier he is!

My feeling of such a man is, he is a great cheat, a deceiver, a liar! He imposes on the people, he takes that which does not belong to him, and is a living monument of falsehood. Such a man is not a financier! The financier is he that brings the lumber from the canyons and shapes it for the use of his fellow man, employing mechanics and laborers to produce from the elements and the crude material everything necessary for the sustenance and comfort of man; one who builds tanneries to work up the hides instead of letting them rot and waste or be sent out of the country to be made into leather and then brought back in the shape of boots and shoes; and that can take the wool, the furs and straw and convert the same into cloth, into hats and bonnets, and that will plant out mulberry trees and raise the silk, and thus give employment to men, women and children, as you have commenced to do here, bringing the elements into successful use for the benefit of man, and reclaiming a barren wilderness, converting it into a fruitful field, making it to blossom as the rose; such a man I would call a financier, a benefactor of his fellow man. But the great majority of men who have amassed great wealth have done it at the expense of their fellows. (*Journal of Discourses* 19:97.)

The course pursued by men of business in the world has a tendency to make a few rich, and to sink the masses of the people in poverty and degradation. (*Journal of Discourses* 11:348.)

Some think too much, and should labor more, others labor too much, and should think more, and thus maintain an equilibrium between the mental and physical members of the individual; then you will enjoy health and vigor, will be active and ready to discern truly, and judge quickly. (*Discourses of Brigham Young*, 261.)

Know whether you ought to do a thing or not, and if you ought not, let it alone. That is the way to live. (*Journal of Discourses* 14:161.)

Do those things that are necessary to be done and let those alone that are not necessary, and we shall accomplish more than we do now. (*Journal of Discourses* 3:160.)

To make ourselves happy is incorporated in the great design of man's existence. I have learned not to fret myself about that which I cannot help. If I can do good, I will do it; and if I cannot reach a thing, I will content myself to be without it. This makes me happy all the day long. (*Discourses of Brigham Young*, 236.)

One-third or one-fourth of the time that is spent to procure a living would be sufficient, if your labor were rightly directed. People think they are going to get rich by hard work—by working sixteen hours out of the twenty-four; but it is not so. A great many of our brethren can hardly spend time to go to meeting. Six days is more time than we need to labor. (*Journal of Discourses* 8:355.)

Work less, wear less, eat less and we shall be a great deal wiser, healthier and wealthier people then by taking the course we now do. (*Discourses of Brigham Young*, 187–88.)

Let us seek to extend the present life to the uttermost, by observing every law of health and by properly balancing labor, study, rest, and recreation and thus prepare for a better life. Let us teach these principles to our children that, in the morning of their days, they may be taught to lay the foundation of health and strength and constitution and power of life in their bodies. (*Discourses of Brigham Young*, 186.)

Of the time that is allotted to man here on the earth there is none to lose or to run to waste. After suitable rest and relaxation there is not a day, hour or minute that we should spend in idleness, but every minute of every day of our lives we should strive to improve our minds and to increase the faith of the holy Gospel, in charity, patience, and good works, that we may grow in the knowledge of the truth as it is spoken and prophesied of and written about. (*Journal of Discourses* 13:310.)

Recreation and diversion are as necessary to our well-being as the more serious pursuits of life. There is not a man in the world but what, if kept at any one branch of business or study, will become like a machine. Our pursuits should be so diversified as to develop every trait of character and diversity of talent. (*Discourses of Brigham Young,* 238–39.)

The non-producer must live on the products of those who labor. There is no other way. If we all labor a few hours a day, we could then spend the remainder of our time in rest and the improvement of our minds. This would give an opportunity to the children to be educated in the learning of the day, and to possess all the wisdom of man. (*Journal of Discourses* 19:47.)

The idler is of no use to himself or to the world in which he dwells. (*Journal of Discourses* 14:83.)

The laboring man, the ingenious, industrious and prudent man, the man who lays himself out to advance the human family in every saving principle for happiness, for beauty and excellency, for wisdom, power, greatness and glory is the true benefactor of this race; he is the gentleman, the honorable, high-minded citizen of the world, and is worthy the society and admiration of the great and wise among all nations, though he may be destitute of wealth and title; he is a civilized man. (*Journal of Discourses* 10:359.)

We want to see a community organized in which every person will be industrious, faithful and prudent. What will you do with the children? We will bring them up until they are of legal age, then say, Go where you please. We have given you a splendid education, the advantage of all the learning of the day, and if you do not wish to stay with the Saints, go where you please. (*Journal of Discourses* 15:226.)

The question will not arise with the Lord, nor with the messengers of the Almighty, how much wealth a man has got, but how has he come by this wealth and what will he do with it? (*Journal of Discourses* 11:294.)

This is as good an earth as need be, if we will make it so. The Lord has redeemed it, and it is his wish that his Saints should beautify and sanctify it and bring it back to the presence of the Father and Son yet more pure, more holy and more excellent than it was in its original state, with ourselves upon it. (*Journal of Discourses,* 10:177.)

This is the counsel I have for the Latter-day Saints today. Stop, do not be in a hurry. I do not know that I could find a man in our community but what wishes wealth, would like to have everything in his possession that would conduce to his comfort and convenience. Do you know how to get it? Well, replies one, if I do not, I wish I did; but I do not seem to be exactly fortunate— fortune is somewhat against me. I will tell you the reason of this—you are in too much of a hurry; you do not go to meeting enough, you do not pray enough, you do not read the Scriptures enough, you do not meditate enough, you are all the time on the wing, and in such a hurry that you do not know what to do first. This is not the way to get rich.

I merely use the term rich to lead the mind along, until we obtain eternal riches in the celestial kingdom of God. Here we wish for riches in a comparative sense, we wish for the comforts of life. If we desire them let us take a course to get them. Let me reduce this to a simple saying—one of the most simple and homely that can be used—Keep your dish right side up, so that when the shower of porridge does come, you can catch your dish full. (*Journal of Discourses* 15:36.)

We are the greatest speculators in the world. We have the greatest speculation on hand that can be found in all the earth. I never denied being a speculator. I never denied being a miser, or of feeling eager for riches; but some men will chase a picayune five thousand miles when I would not turn round for it, and yet we are preachers of the same Gospel, and brethren in the same Kingdom of God. You may consider this is a little strong; but the speculation I am after, is to exchange this world, which, in its present state, passes away, for a world that is eternal and unchangeable, for a glorified world filled with eternal riches, for the world that is made an inheritance for the Gods of eternity. (*Journal of Discourses* 1:326.)

Though our time be entirely occupied in laboring for the advancement of the Kingdom of God on the earth we are in reality laboring most effectually for self, for all our interest and welfare, both in time and eternity, are circumscribed and bound up in that Kingdom. (*Discourses of Brigham Young,* 231.)

When men act upon the principles which will secure to them eternal salvation, they are sure of obtaining all their hearts' desire, sooner or later; if it does not come today, it may come tomorrow; if it does not come in this time, it will in the next. (*Journal of Discourses* 2:122.)

Whether we are raising cattle, planting, gathering, building, or inhabiting, we are in the Lord, and all we do is within the pale of His kingdom upon the earth, consequently it is all spiritual and all temporal, no matter what we are laboring to accomplish. (*Journal of Discourses,* 10:329.)

We say to the Latter-day Saints, work for these capitalists, and work honestly and faithfully, and they will pay you faithfully. I am acquainted with a good many of them, and as far as I know them, I do not know but every one is an honorable man. They are capitalists, they want to make money, and they want to make it honestly and according to the principles of honest dealing. If they have means and are determined to risk it in opening mines you work for them by the day. Haul their ores, build their furnaces and take your pay for it, and enter your lands, build houses, improve your farms, buy your stock, and make yourselves better off. (*Journal of Discourses* 14:85.)

Now, brethren, what do you say, will you do as I want you to? Will you take hold and build this meeting-house, get this road through and make a little more improvement, and say we will have no idlers in our midst, but that every day, every week, every month, shall be devoted to something that is useful to ourselves and to others? (*Journal of Discourses* 16:70-71.)

Will you do this? "Aye, maybe I will," says one, and "maybe I wont" says another; "the kingdom that cannot support me I don't think of much account; the Lord has said it is his business to provide for his Saints, and I guess he will do it." I have no doubt but what he will provide for his Saints; but if you do not take this counsel and be industrious and prudent, you will not long continue to be one of his Saints. (*Journal of Discourses* 11:105-106.)

Covetousness

I am more afraid of covetousness in our Elders than I am of the hordes of hell. (*Journal of Discourses* 5:353.)

I would as soon see a man worshipping a little god made of brass or of wood as to see him worship his property. (*Journal of Discourses* 6:196.)

Do you not know that the possession of your property is like a shadow, or the dew of the morning before the noonday sun, that you cannot have any assurance of its control for a single moment! It is the unseen hand of Providence that controls it. (*Journal of Discourses* 1:114.)

Look out, ye men of Israel, and be careful that you love not the world or the things of the world in their present state, and in your loftiness and pride, forget the Lord your God. We ought to care no more for the silver and the gold, and the property that is so much sought for by the wicked world, than for the soil or the gravel upon which we tread. (*Journal of Discourses* 11:18.)

Let us not love the things of this world above the things of God, but strip for the race and harness for the battle of the Gospel plan of salvation. (*Discourses of Brigham Young,* 231.)

I see men and women in this congregation—only a few of them—who were driven from the central Stake of Zion [in Jackson County, Missouri]. Ask them if they had any sorrow or trouble; then let them look at the beautiful land that the Lord would have given them if all had been faithful in keeping his commandments, and had walked before him as they should; and then ask them with regard to the blessings they would have received. If they tell you the sentiments of their minds, they will tell you that the yoke of Jesus would have been easy and his burden would have been light, and that it would have been a delightful task to have walked in obedience to his commandments and to have been of one heart and one mind; but through the selfishness of some, which is idolatry, through their covetousness, which is the same, and the lustful desire of their minds, they were cast out and driven from their homes. (*Discourses of Brigham Young,* 113–14.)

Men are greedy for the vain things of this world. In their hearts they are covetous. It is true that the things of this world are designed to make us comfortable, and they make some people as happy as they can be here; but riches can never make the Latter-day Saints happy. Riches of themselves cannot produce permanent happiness; only the Spirit that comes from above can do that. (*Journal of Discourses* 7:135.)

Those who are covetous and greedy, anxious to grasp the whole world, are all the time uneasy, and are constantly laying their plans and contriving how to obtain this, that, and the other. (*Journal of Discourses* 3:119.)

Envy not those who do better than you do; do not pursue them with malice, but try to shape and frame your life by theirs. (*Discourses of Brigham Young,* 272.)

We wish to know a great deal, and do not want our neighbors to know as much as we do, but wish them to believe that we know it all. This trait of character is very common, both here and through the whole world. We all wish to know something that our neighbors do not know. With scientific men you will often find the same trait of character "My studies and my researches are beyond those of my neighbors; I know more than they know; I treasure this up to myself, and I am looked upon as a superior being, and that delights me." I say to the Latter-day Saints, and to all the world, this is all wrong. (*Journal of Discourses* 17:52.)

If the Lord ever revealed anything to me, he has shown me that the Elders of Israel must let speculation alone and attend to the duties of their calling, otherwise they will have little or no power in their missions or upon their return. (*Journal of Discourses* 8:179.)

How the Devil will play with a man who so worships gain! (*Journal of Discourses* 10:174.)

These are a few words of consolation to the brethren who wish to keep their riches, and with them I promise you leanness of soul, darkness of mind, narrow and contracted hearts, and the bowels of your compassion will be shut up, and by and by you will be overcome with the spirit of apostasy and forsake your God and your brethren. (*Journal of Discourses* 12:127.)

The Latter-day Saints who turn their attention to money-making soon become cold in their feelings toward the ordinances of the house of God. They neglect their prayers, become unwilling to pay any donations; the law of tithing gets too great a task for them; and they finally forsake their God, and the providences of heaven seem to be shut from them—all in consequence of this lust after the things of this world, which will certainly perish in handling, and in their use they will fade away and go from us. (*Journal of Discourses* 18:213.)

Men and women who are trying to make themselves happy in the possession of wealth or power will miss it, for nothing short of the Gospel of the Son of God can make the inhabitants of the earth happy, and prepare them to enjoy heaven here and hereafter. (*Journal of Discourses* 11:329.)

Do not be anxious to have this people become rich, and possess the affection of the world. I have been fearful lest we come to fellowship the world. (*Journal of Discourses* 10:298.)

The worst fear that I have about this people is that they will get rich in this country, forget God and his people, wax fat, and kick themselves out of the Church and go to hell. This people will stand mobbing, robbing, poverty, and all manner of persecution, and be true. But my greater fear for them is that they cannot stand wealth; and yet they have to be tried with riches, for they will become the richest people on this earth. (*Brigham Young: The Man and His Work,* 127–28.)

Never pray for riches; do not entertain such a foolish thought. In my deep poverty, when I knew not where I could procure the next morsel of food for myself and family, I have prayed God to open the way that I might get something to keep myself and family from dying. Those who do more than this are off, more or less, from the track that leads to life eternal. (*Journal of Discourses* 7:138.)

It is thought by many that the possession of gold and silver will produce for them happiness, and, hence, thousands hunt the mountains for the precious metals; in this they are mistaken. The possession of wealth alone does not produce happiness, although it will produce comfort, when it can be exchanged for the essentials and luxuries of life. When wealth is obtained by purloining, or in any other unfair and dishonorable way, fear of detection and punishment robs the possessor of all human happiness. When wealth is honorably obtained by man, still the possession of it is embittered by the thought that death will soon strip them of it and others will possess it. What hopes have they in the future, after they get through with this sorrowful world? They know nothing about the future; they see nothing but death and hell. Solid comfort and unalloyed joy are unknown to them. (*Journal of Discourses* 11:15.)

Some say, If we had a gold mine, we would do well. If I knew where there was a gold mine, I would not tell you. I do not want you to find one, and I do not mean that you shall; or, if you do, it shall be over my faith. We have gold enough in the world, and it is all the Lord's, and we do not deserve more than we get. Let us make good use of that, and send out the Elders. (*Journal of Discourses* 8:204.)

What use is gold when you get enough to eat, drink, and wear without it? (*Journal of Discourses* 1:250.)

The whole world are after happiness. It is not found in gold and silver, but it is in peace and love. (*Discourses of Brigham Young*, 235.)

The possession of all the gold and silver in the world would not satisfy the cravings of the immortal soul of man. The gift of the Holy Spirit of the Lord alone can produce a good, wholesome, contented mind. Instead of looking for gold and silver, look to the heavens and try to learn wisdom until you can organize the native elements for your benefit; then, and not until then, will you begin to possess the true riches. (*Discourses of Brigham Young*, 305.)

There is no happiness in gold, not in the least. It is very convenient as an article of exchange, in purchasing what we need; and instead of finding comfort and happiness in gold, you exchange it to obtain happiness, or that which may conduce to it. There is no real wealth in gold. People talk about being wealthy—about being rich; but place the richest banking company in the world upon a barren rock, with their gold piled around them, with no possible chance of exchanging it, and destitute of the creature comforts, and they would be poor indeed. Where then is their joy, their comfort, their great wealth? They have none. (*Journal of Discourses* 8:168.)

We are not anxious to obtain gold; if we can obtain it by raising potatoes and wheat, all right. Can't you make yourselves rich by speculating? We do not wish to. Can't you make yourselves rich by going to the gold mines? We are right in the midst of them. Why don't you dig the gold from the earth? Because it demoralizes any community or nation on the earth to give them gold and silver to their hearts' content; it will ruin any nation. But give them iron and coal, good hard work, plenty to eat, good schools and good doctrine, and it will make them a healthy, wealthy and happy people. (*Journal of Discourses* 13:176.)

The time will come that gold will hold no comparison in value to a bushel of wheat. (*Journal of Discourses* 1:250.)

What have you to give? Some will say, "I have not anything, brother Brigham." "What have you been doing?" "Oh, I have been mining, and it takes all my time and labor to support my family. I have a splendid claim—I am just going to have a hundred thousand dollars for it." We have plenty of this class around, and whenever I see a man going along with an old mule that can hardly stand up, and a frying pan and an old quilt, I say, There

goes a millionaire in prospect! He is after a million, he calculates
to find a mine that he can get a million for next summer.

These millionaires are all over our country; they are in the
mountains, on our highways and in our streets. But ask them,
"Can you give me a sixpence to buy me a morsel of meat?" "No,
I have not got it, I am just going to have plenty of money, but
I have not got it now. Cannot you lend me a little to keep me
from need, I have no bread for my family, but I am going to have
a fortune in a little while."

There are numbers of the Elders of Israel in this position. Ask
them if they can pay a little tithing? "No, not a dollar." "Give
anything to help the poor?" "No, I have not any, will you lend
me a little to buy some flour for my family?" And so they go
on year after year. Why? Because they will not take the counsel
of the wise. . . .

Just think of these men, trailing through these canyons, running after shadows—jack-o'lanterns—all over creation for something in prospect! They are just like some business men I have
seen in my life—they have got their eye on a picayune, away off
yonder in the distance, and they start after that and stub their
toe against a twenty dollar gold piece; but they kick that out of
the way, they do not see it. By and by they start again, and they
pass fifty dollars in their path, and so they keep on, passing right
by ten, twenty or fifty dollars. "Oh, that picayune does so dazzle
my eye, for God's sake let me get it!" They are fools, they know
nothing about life, nor sustaining themselves, they are worse
than children. (*Journal of Discourses* 16:22–23.)

The possession of wealth alone does not produce happiness,
although it will produce comfort, when it can be exchanged for
the essentials and luxuries of life. When wealth is obtained by
purloining, or in any other unfair and dishonorable way, fear
of detection and punishment robs the possessor of all human
happiness. When wealth is honorably obtained by man, still the
possession of it is embittered by the thought that death will soon

strip them of it and others will possess it. What hopes have they in the future, after they get through with this sorrowful world? They know nothing about the future; they see nothing but death and hell. Solid comfort and unalloyed joy are unknown to them. (*Discourses of Brigham Young,* 314.)

If you were in possession of all the wealth in the world, it is not worth so much to you as your good characters. (*Journal of Discourses,* 8:346.)

Let wisdom be sown in your hearts, and let it bring forth a bountiful harvest. It is more profitable to you than all the gold and silver and other riches of earth. Let wisdom spring up in your hearts, and cultivate it. (*Discourses of Brigham Young,* 261.)

❖ *Chapter the Second* ❖

USING WEALTH

Waste Not, Want Not

Never let anything go to waste. Be prudent, save everything, and what you get more than you can take care of yourselves, ask your neighbors to help you consume. (*Journal of Discourses* 1:250.)

Idleness and wastefulness are not according to the rules of heaven. Preserve all you can, that you may have abundance to bless your friends and your enemies. (*Journal of Discourses* 14:44.)

Study order and cleanliness in your various occupations. Adorn your city and neighbourhood. Make your homes lovely, and adorn your hearts with the grace of God. (*Journal of Discourses* 8:297.)

I have passed much of my life in a log-house, but do I like bed-bugs and darkness? No. I love light. Were I obliged to live in a log-house, I would have it plastered and whitewashed, that it might be neat and pleasant. (*Journal of Discourses* 8:297.)

Do not put your shoes under the stove to burn up, and when you undress at night do not fling your hat one way, your jacket another, your breeches under foot, and your stockings under the stove, on the stove, or out of doors, but have a place for everything, and everything in its place. (*Journal of Discourses* 11:352.)

Were I now to go into one of your houses, perhaps I should hear the mistress inquiring for the dishcloth; but Sal does not know where it is: the last she saw of it little Abraham or joe was playing with it outdoors. Where is the milk-pail? Turned bottom-side up on the hog-pen. (*Journal of Discourses* 8:296.)

Mother gets up and it is: "O, Sally, where is the dish cloth, I want it in a minute?" "Susan, where in the world have you put that broom?" or, "Where is the iron holder?" and Susan knows nothing about either dish cloth or broom, and says, "We have no iron holder except some waste paper." If I had nothing but a piece of an old newspaper folded for a holder I would have it where I could put my hand on it in a moment, in the dark if I wanted it. And so with the dishcloth, the broom, the chairs, tables, sofas, and everything about the house, so that if you had to get up in the night you could lay your hand on whatever you wanted instantly. Have a place for everything and everything in its place. (*Journal of Discourses* 14:89.)

When a farmer has done with his ploughs, he should put them under shelter until they are again wanted. When harness is taken off, it should be so hung up that you can go at any time of night and find it, or a saddle, bridle, saddle-blanket, or any other trapping, and be ready at once. (*Journal of Discourses* 8:296.)

I may go to a house and what do I see? Perhaps the bottom or top of the bread is burnt to coal. Why did you not do different? "O, these are accidents." Yes, because we never think of the business on our hands. (*Journal of Discourses* 14:88-89.)

I have been into houses which have not had the least convenience for the women, not so much as a bench to set their water pails on, and they have to set them on the floor, and yet their husbands will sit there year after year, and never make so much improvement as a bench to set the pail on. Yet they have the ability, but they will not exercise it. (*Discourses of Brigham Young,* 198–99.)

You may see some little girls around the streets here with their mothers' skirts on, or their sun bonnets, and with their aprons full of dirt. Your husbands buy you calico, but you do not know what to do with it. It is to be carefully worn until the last thread is worn out, and then put into the rag bag to make paper with. (*Journal of Discourses* 4:319.)

Everything which we use to feed the life of man or beast, not a grain of it should be permitted to go to waste, but should be made to pass through the stomach of some animal; everything, also, which will fertilize our gardens and our fields should be sedulously saved and wisely husbanded, that nothing may be lost which contains the elements of food and raiment for man and sustenance for beast. (*Journal of Discourses* 11:130.)

Never consider that you have bread enough around you to suffer your children to waste a crust or a crumb of it. If a man is worth millions of bushels of wheat and corn, he is not wealthy enough to suffer his servant girl to sweep a single kernel of it into the fire; let it be eaten by something and pass again into the earth, and thus fulfil the purpose for which it grew. Remember it, do not waste anything, but take care of everything. (*Journal of Discourses* 1:253.)

There is not a family in this city, where there are two, three, four, or five persons, but what can save enough from their table, from the waste made by the children, and what must be swept in the fire and out of the door, to make pork sufficient to last them through the year, or at least all they should eat. (*Journal of Discourses* 4:314.)

Take things calm and easy, pick up everything, let nothing go to waste. (*Journal of Discourses* 14:88.)

If the Lord gives good crops this season, and tells us to lay up from that abundance, I do not think He will increase His blessings upon us if we foolishly squander those He has already given us. (*Journal of Discourses,* 12:219.)

Putting Wealth to Work

The first revelation given to Adam was of a temporal nature. Most of the revelations he received pertained to his life here. That was also the case in the revelations to Noah. We have but very few of the instructions the Lord gave to Enoch, concerning his city; but, doubtless, most of the revelations he received pertained to a temporal nature and condition. And certainly the revelations Noah received, so far as in our possession, almost exclusively pertained to this life. The same principle was carried out in the days of Moses, and in the days of his fathers, Abraham, Isaac, and Jacob. We may say that eight or nine-tenths of the doctrines and principles set forth in the revelations given to those men were of a temporal nature.

[The Lord's] labor is to build up, not to destroy; to gather together, not to scatter abroad; to take the ignorant and lead them to wisdom; to pick up the poor and bring them to comfortable circumstances. This is our labor—what we have to do. (*Discourses of Brigham Young,* 427.)

If you wish to get rich, save what you get. A fool can earn money; but it takes a wise man to save and dispose of it to his own advantage. (*Journal of Discourses* 11:301.)

Our wants are many, but our real necessities are very few. Let us govern our wants by our necessities, and we shall find that we are not compelled to spend our money for naught. Let us save our money to enter and pay for our land, to buy flocks of sheep and improve them, and to buy machinery and start more woolen factories. (*Journal of Discourses* 12:289.)

Few men know what to do with riches when they possess them. (*Journal of Discourses* 1:250.)

If, by industrious habits and honorable dealings, you obtain thousands or millions, little or much, it is your duty to use all that is put in your possession, as judiciously as you have knowledge, to build up the Kingdom of God on the earth. (*Journal of Discourses* 4:29.)

I am not for hoarding up gold and other property to lie useless, I wish to put everything to a good use. I never keep a dollar lying idly by me, for I wish all the means to be put into active operation. (*Journal of Discourses* 3:160.)

A man has no right with property, which, according to the laws of the land, legally belongs to him, if he does not want to use it; he ought to possess no more than he can put to usury, and cause to do good to himself and his fellow man. When will a man accumulate money enough to justify him in salting it down, or, in other words, laying it away in the chest, to lock it up, there to lie, doing no manner of good either to himself or his neighbor? It is impossible for a man ever to do it.

No man should keep money or property by him that he cannot put to usury for the advancement of that property in value or amount, and for the good of the community in which he lives; if he does, it becomes a dead weight upon him. Every man who has got cattle, money, or wealth of any description, bone and sinew, should put it out to usury. If a man has the arm, body, head, the component parts of a system to constitute him a laboring man, and has nothing in the world to depend upon but his hands, let him put them to usury. Never hide up anything in a napkin, but put it forth to bring an increase. If you have got property of any kind, that you do not know what to do with, lay it out in making a farm, or building a sawmill or a woolen factory, and go to with your mights to put all your property to usury.

I told you the other day what makes me rich, it is the labor of those whom I feed and clothe; still I do not feel that I have a dollar in the world that is my own, it is the Lord's and he has made me a steward over it; and if I can know where the Lord is pleased to have it appropriated, there it shall go. (*Journal of Discourses* 3:118.)

I like to see men get rich by their industry, prudence, management and economy, and then devote it to the building up of the kingdom of God upon the earth, and in gathering in the poor saints from the four comers of the earth; and I am pleased to say that our rich brethren are doing well. (*Journal of Discourses* 11:115.)

Gold is good in its place—it is good in the hands of good men to do good with, but in the hands of a wicked man it often proves a curse instead of a blessing. Gold is a good servant, but a miserable, blind, and helpless god, and at last will have to be purified by fire, with all its followers. (*Messages of the First Presidency*, 2:46.)

I do not care what becomes of the things of this world, of the gold, of the silver, of the houses and of the lands, so we have power to gather the House of Israel, redeem Zion, and establish the Kingdom of God on the earth. I would not give a cent for all the rest. True, these things which the Lord bestows upon us are for our comfort, for our happiness and convenience, but everything must be devoted to the upbuilding of the Kingdom of God on the earth. (*Journal of Discourses* 3:361.)

If a man comes in the midst of this people with money, let him use it in beautifying his inheritance in Zion, and in increasing his capital by thus putting out his money to usury. Let him go and make a great farm, and stock it well, and fortify all around with a good and efficient fence. What for? Why for the purpose of spending his money. Then let him cut it up into fields, and adorn it with trees, and build a fine house upon it. What for? Why, for the purpose of spending his money. What will he do when his money is gone? The money thus spent, with a wise and prudent hand, is in a situation to accumulate and increase a hundred-fold.

When he has done making his farm, and his means still increase by his diligent use of it, he can then commence and build a woolen factory for instance; he can send and buy the sheep and have them brought here, and have them herded here, and shear them here, and take care of them, then set the boys and girls to cleaning, carding, spinning, and weaving the wool into cloth, and thus employ hundreds and thousands of the brethren and sisters who have come from the manufacturing districts of the old country, and have not been accustomed to dig in the earth for their livelihood, who have not learned anything else but to work in the factory. This would feed them and clothe them, and put within their reach the comforts of life; it would also create at home a steady market for the produce of the agriculturist, and the labor of the mechanic. (*Journal of Discourses* 1:253.)

If I improve upon what the Lord has given me, and continue to improve, I shall become like those who have gone before me; I shall be exalted in the celestial kingdom, and be filled to overflowing with all the power I can wield; and all the keys of knowledge I can manage will be committed unto me. (*Discourses of Brigham Young*, 460.)

If we are destroyed through the possession of wealth, it will be because we destroy ourselves. If we possessed hundreds of millions of coin and devoted that means to building up the Kingdom of God and doing good to his creatures, with an eye single to his glory, we would be as much blessed and as much entitled to salvation as the poor beggar that begs from door to door; the faithful rich man is as much entitled to the revelations of Jesus Christ as is the faithful poor man. (*Journal of Discourses* 10:300.)

If you wish to gain power in the minds of any people, give them the same opportunity that you possess to become independent and self-sustaining, and endow them with all the wisdom and knowledge that they are capable of receiving, and let them increase with you and unitedly grow and become strong. (*Discourses of Brigham Young,* 357–58.)

Instead of people being poor, we already have too much, unless we take better care of it. I heard a man who is living in this city—one who has always been well off—state that he used to keep twelve cows when he first came here, and was often nearly destitute of milk and butter. After a few years, the number of his cows was reduced to six, and he said that the six did him more good than the twelve had done. In two years more, they were reduced to two, and the two cows have done him much more good than the twelve or the six did, for they could be and were more properly attended to. (*Journal of Discourses* 4:317.)

If you have more oxen and other cattle than you need, put them in the hands of other men, and receive their labor in return, and put that labor where it will increase your property value. (*Journal of Discourses* 1:252.)

It has been supposed that wealth gives power. In a depraved state of society, in a certain sense it does, if opening a wide field for unrighteous monopolies, by which the poor are robbed and oppressed and the wealthy are more enriched, is power. In a depraved state of society money can buy positions and titles, can cover up a multitude of incapabilities, can open wide the gates of fashionable society to the lowest and most depraved of human beings; it divides society into castes without any reference to goodness, virtue or truth. It is made to pander to the most brutal passions of the human soul; it is made to subvert every wholesome law of God and man, and to trample down every sacred bond that should tie society together in a national, municipal, domestic and every other relationship. Wealth thus used is used out of its legitimate channel. (*Journal of Discourses* 10:3.)

It is against my doctrine and feelings for men to scrape together the wealth of the world and let it waste and do no good. (*Journal of Discourses* 9:186.)

It is good policy and economy to sustain each other. (*Journal of Discourses* 12:63.)

It is much better to be honest; to live here uprightly, and forsake and shun evil, than it is to be dishonest. It is the easiest path in the world to be honest,—to be upright before God; and when people learn this, they will practice it. (*Discourses of Brigham Young,* 232.)

If we accept salvation on the terms it is offered to us, we have got to be honest in every thought, in our reflections, in our meditations, in our private circles, in our deals, in our declarations, and in every act of our lives, fearless and regardless of every principle of error, of every principle of falsehood that may be presented. (*Discourses of Brigham Young,* 389.)

Let us . . . live so as to create confidence in all men with whom we deal and come in contact; and treasure up each particle of confidence we obtain as one of the most precious possessions mortals can possibly possess. When by my good actions I have created confidence in my neighbor towards me, I pray that I may never do anything that will destroy it. (*Discourses of Brigham Young,* 276.)

The time is coming when a good man will be more precious than fine gold. (*Journal of Discourses,* 10:294–95.)

To do right can be reduced to perfect simplicity in a few words, viz., from this time henceforth, let no person work, or transact any kind of business whatever, that he cannot do in the name of the Lord. (*Journal of Discourses* 1:337.)

There is any amount of property, and gold and silver in the earth and on the earth, and the Lord gives to this one and that one—the wicked as well as the righteous—to see what they will do with it, but it all belongs to him. He has handed over a goodly portion to this people, and, through our faith, patience and industry, we have made us good, comfortable homes here, and there are many who are tolerably well off, and if they were in many parts of the world they would be called wealthy. But it is not ours, and all we have to do is to try and find out what the Lord wants us to do with what we have in our possession, and then go and do it. If we step beyond this, or to the right or to the left, we step into an illegitimate train of business. Our legitimate business is to do what the Lord wants us to do with that which he bestows upon us, and dispose of it just as he dictates, whether it is to give all, one-tenth, or the surplus. (*Journal of Discourses* 16:10.)

It is not for me to rise up and say that I can give to the Lord, for in reality I have nothing to give. I seem to have something. Why? Because the Lord has seen fit to bring me forth, and has blessed my efforts in gathering things which are desirable, and which are termed property. (*Journal of Discourses* 2:300.)

It is to our advantage to take good care of the blessings God bestows upon us; if we pursue the opposite course, we cut off the power and glory God designs we should inherit. It is through our own carefulness, frugality, and judgment which God has given us, that we are enabled to preserve our grain, our flocks and herds, wives and children, houses and lands, and increase them around us, continually gaining power and influence for ourselves as individuals and for the Kingdom of God as a whole. (*Journal of Discourses* 9:171.)

Latter-day Saints . . . should not suffer reverses and unpleasant circumstances to sour their natures and render them fretful and unsocial at home, speaking words full of bitterness . . . to their wives and children, creating gloom and sorrow in their habitations, making themselves feared rather than beloved by their families. (*Discourses of Brigham Young,* 203–4.)

It is your right, wives, to ask your husbands to set out beautiful shade and fruit trees, and to get you some vines and flowers with which to adorn the outside of your dwellings; and if your husbands have not time, get them yourselves and plant them out. Some, perhaps, will say, "Oh, I have nothing but a log house, and it is not worth that." Yes; it is worth it. Whitewash and plaster it up, and get vines to run over the door, so that everybody who passes will say, "What a lovely little cottage!" This is your privilege and I wish you to exercise yourselves in your own rights. (*Discourses of Brigham Young,* 200.)

Let the husband make an improvement upon his kitchen and pantry and upon his bedrooms for the benefit of his family, and improve his gardens, walks, etc, beautifying your habitations and their surroundings, making pavements and planting shade trees. (*Discourses of Brigham Young,* 198.)

It is the business of a Latter-day Saint, in passing through the street, if he sees a fence pole down, to put it up; if he sees an animal in the mud to stop and help get it out. (*Discourses of Brigham Young,* 427.)

Let mechanics and every man who has capital create business and give employment and means into the hands of laborers; build good and commodious houses, magnificent temples, spacious tabernacles, lofty halls, and every other kind of structure that will give character and grandeur to our cities and create respect for our people. Let us make mechanics of our boys, and educate them in every useful branch of science and in the history and laws of kingdoms and nations, that they may be fitted to fill any station in life, from a plough man to a philosopher. (*Journal of Discourses* 10:270.)

Now, cultivate your farms and gardens well, and drive your stock to where they can live through the winter, if you have not feed for them. Do not keep so many cattle, or, in other words, more than you can well provide for and make profitable to yourselves and to the Kingdom of God. We have hundreds and thousands of fat cattle upon the ranges, and yet we have no beef to eat, or very little. Kill your cattle when they are fat, and salt down the meat, that you may have meat to eat in the winter and some to dispose of to your neighbors for their labor to extend your improvements. Lay up your meat, and not let it die on your hands. Such a course is not right. Cattle are made for our use, let us take care of them. (*Journal of Discourses* 11:142.)

Purchase cows, for if we have not already supplied you with cows, we are able and willing to do so. Most, if not all, have already been furnished with cows. What did you do with the calves? We sold them for a trifle. Why did you not raise them? Do you not know that they would very soon be valuable? No, but you waste your calves, neglect buying pigs, and live without milk, and many of the easily procured comforts of life. (*Journal of Discourses* 4:315.)

Save your hay; save your chaff; save your straw; save your wheat; save your oats; save your barley, and everything that can be saved and preserved against a day of want. (*Journal of Discourses* 12:241.)

Save your wool, and send it to the factory. If we want a little cotton cloth, we can raise it in the southern country; and we could raise some here as well as in some other places. We can raise about two gatherings. (*Journal of Discourses* 19:73.)

The capitalists may say, What are we to do with our means? Go and build factories and have one, two, or three thousand spindles going. Send for fifty, a hundred, or a thousand sheep and raise wool. Some of you go to raising flax and build a factory to manufacture it, and do not take every advantage and pocket every dollar that is to be made. You are rich and I want to turn the stream so as to do good to the whole community. (*Journal of Discourses* 13:36.)

The great majority of men and women do not know how to take care of themselves. Let me refer the whole of you to a circumstance in Winter Quarters. We left Nauvoo in February, 1846, made our own roads through Iowa, except some 40 or 50 miles, built bridges, cut down timber, turned out 500 men to go to Mexico, came this side of the Missouri river, and there wintered. How did you live there? Do you know how you got anything to eat? Brethren came to me, saying, We must go to Missouri. Can we not take our families and go to Missouri, and get work? Do you know, to this day, how you lived? I will tell you, and then you will remember it. I had not five dollars in money to start with; but I went to work and built a mill, which I knew we should want only for a few months, that cost 3,600 dollars. I gave notice that I would employ every man and pay him for his labor. If I had a sixpence, I turned it into 25 cents; and a half-bushel of potatoes I turned into a half-a-bushel of wheat. How did I do that? By faith. I went to Brother Neff, who had just come in the place, and asked him for and received 2,600 dollars, though he did not know where the money was going. He kept the mill another year, and it died on his hands. I say, God bless him forever! for it was the money he brought from Pennsylvania that preserved thousands of men, women, and children from starving. I handled and dictated it, and everything went off smoothly and prosperously. (*Journal of Discourses* 6:173.)

The increase of our children, and their growing up to maturity, increases our responsibilities. More land must be brought into cultivation to supply their wants. This will press the necessity of digging canals to guide the waters of our large streams over the immense tracts of bench and bottom lands which now lie waste. We want our children to remain near us, where there is an abundance of land and water, and not go hundreds of miles away to seek homes. In these great public improvements the people should enter with heart and soul, and freely invest in them their surplus property and means, and thus prepare to locate the vast multitudes of our children which are growing up, and strengthen our hands, and solidify still more—make still more compact our present organized spiritual and national institutions. (*Journal of Discourses* 11:116.)

The property which we inherit from our Heavenly Father is our time, and the power to choose in the disposition of the same. This is the real capital that is bequeathed unto us by our Heavenly Father; all the rest is what he may be pleased to add unto us. (*Journal of Discourses,* 18:354.)

What have we? Our time. Spend it as you will. Time is given to you; and when this is spent to the best possible advantage for promoting truth upon the earth, it is placed to our account, and blessed are you; but when we spend our time in idleness and folly it will be placed against us. (*Journal of Discourses* 19:75.)

We have to give an account of the days we spend in folly. (*Journal of Discourses* 19:75.)

This is the greatest wealth we possess—to know how to direct our labors rightly, spending every hour advantageously. (*Journal of Discourses* 12:172.)

Time and the ability to labor are the capital stock of the whole world of mankind, and we are all indebted to God for the ability to use time to advantage, and he will require of us a strict account of the disposition we make of this ability; and he will not only require an account of our acts, but our words and thoughts will also be brought into judgment. (*Journal of Discourses* 18:73.)

This life is worth as much as any life that any being can possess in time or in eternity. There is no life more precious to us in the eye of eternal wisdom and justice than the life which we now possess. Our first duty is to take care of this life. (*Journal of Discourses* 11:113.)

There is no lasting pleasure here, unless it is in God. (*Journal of Discourses,* 18:213.)

Though I possessed millions of money and property, that does not excuse me from performing the labor that it is my calling to perform, so far as I have strength and ability, any more than the poorest man in the community is excused. The more we are blessed with means, the more we are blessed with responsibility; the more we are blessed with wisdom and ability, the more we are placed under the necessity of using that wisdom and ability in the spread of righteousness, the subjugation of sin and misery, and the amelioration of the condition of mankind. The man that has only one talent and the man that has five talents have responsibility accordingly. If we have a world of means, we have a world of responsibility. If we have an eternity of knowledge, we shall have an eternity of business to transact and to occupy every particle of the knowledge bestowed upon us. (*Journal of Discourses* 9:172.)

Then do not hoard up your gold; if you do, it will canker, but put out every dollar to usury. Instead of your souls being bound up in your cattle and other property, put it all where it should be placed for the benefit of the Kingdom of God on earth and for his glory. (*Journal of Discourses* 9:191.)

To be prudent and saving, and to use the elements in our possession for our benefit and the benefit of our fellow beings is wise and righteous; but to be slothful, wasteful, lazy and indolent, to spend our time and means for naught, is unrighteous. (*Journal of Discourses* 16:16.)

Train up your children to be beautiful and fair. . . . Let the sisters take care of themselves, and make themselves beautiful, and if any of you are so superstitious and ignorant as to say that this is pride, I can say that you are not informed as to the pride which is sinful before the Lord, you are also ignorant as to the excellency of the heavens, and of the beauty which dwells in the society of the Gods. Were you to see an angel, you would see a beautiful and lovely creature. Make yourselves like angels in goodness and beauty. (*Journal of Discourses* 12:201-202.)

When you come down stairs look as if you were wide awake, and not as if your eyes needed a dish of water to wash them clear and clean. (*Journal of Discourses* 16:21.)

If I am washed and made clean, if I am attired in comely garments, or there is anything extra upon me to beautify, it is considered by some as the height of folly and pride; it is looked upon as a sin of the deepest dye; and the feeling arises, "If I could believe such a gentleman or lady to be a Christian, I should despair of the good that is with me." Why? "Because I have been taught that all this is pride." (*Journal of Discourses* 9:123.)

You see some persons who appear at meetings on the Sabbath and on other public occasions with their hair uncombed and their faces, hands, and clothing uncleanly. Have they no combs nor soap? They have, or can get them. How happens it that we behold such conduct? Probably the parents of those persons taught them that it was pride that prompted people to appear clean and decent. Perhaps their mothers taught them in their infancy that if they washed their faces, and combed and anointed their hair, and dressed themselves in comely apparel to appear before their fellow-men, "Oh, you are full of pride!" Sisters, were not some of you taught in your youth that if you wore a silk dress, you did so purely through pride? Many of you were. I knew one sister in this Church who burned up several dresses when she became a Methodist, because she thought it not right for her to wear rich and costly clothing; that pride prompted costly dress, and in it she could not come before the Lord in humility. She also thought that if she gave her rich dresses away, others would commit the same sin that she would commit in wearing them; so she destroyed them. (*Journal of Discourses* 9:121-122.)

Use good language, wear comely clothing and act in all things so that you can respect yourselves and respect each other. (*Journal of Discourses* 12:300.)

Use just enough of your earnings to make your bodies and your families happy and comfortable, and save the residue. (*Journal of Discourses* 9:295.)

Cleanliness and neatness of person are desirable and good to see, but this may be carried to an extreme that is both tiresome and expensive; there is a class that is more nice than wise. (*Journal of Discourses* 10:29.)

We cannot trust to the certainty of mortal possessions; they are transitory, and a dependence upon them will plunge into hopeless disappointment all those who trust in them. (*Journal of Discourses* 2:122.)

We must watch and pray, and look well to our walk and conversation, and live near to our God, that the love of this world may not choke the precious seed of truth, and feel ready, if necessary, to offer up all things, even life itself, for the Kingdom of Heaven's sake. (*Journal of Discourses* 11:111.)

We own nothing but the talents God has given to us to improve upon, to show him what we will do with them. (*Journal of Discourses* 8:293.)

We should find that the things of this world called riches, are in reality not riches. We should find they are like mirages to the ignorant, mere phenomena to the inhabitants of the earth; today they are, to-morrow they are not; they were, but now they are gone, it is not known where. The earthly king upon his throne, who reigns triumphantly over his subjects, is blasted, with all his kingdom, and brought to naught at one breath of him who possesses true riches. Let him who possesses the true riches say to the elements around that kingdom, produce no wheat, nor oil, nor wine, but let there be a famine upon that people, in such a circumstance where is the wealth of that king, his power, his grandeur, and his crown? There is no bread, no oil, there are no flocks, no herds, for they have perished upon the plains, his wheat is blasted, and all his crops are mildewed. What good does his wealth do him? His subjects are lying all around him lifeless for want of bread; he may cry to them, but in vain; his wealth, power, and influence have vanished, they are swept away like the flimsy fabric of a cobweb. (*Journal of Discourses* 1:266.)

What I have in my mind with regard to this co-operative business is this: There are very few people who cannot get twenty-five dollars to put into one of these co-operative stores. There are hundreds and thousands of women who, by prudence and industry, can obtain this sum. And we say to you, put your capital into one of these stores. What for? To bring you interest for your money. Put your time and talents to usury. We have the parable before us. If we have one, two, three or five talents, of what advantage will they be if we wrap them in a napkin and lay them away? None at all. Put them out to usury. These co-operative stores are instituted to give the poor a little advantage as well as the rich. (*Journal of Discourses* 12:375.)

Whatsoever administers to the sustenance, comfort and health of mankind forms the basis of the commerce of the world. Gold and silver in coin are only valuable as mediums to facilitate exchange. They can be made useful to us and add to our comfort when made into cups, plates, etc., in our household economy. (*Journal of Discourses* 10:227.)

When a man wishes to give anything, let him give the best he has got. The Lord has given to me all I possess; I have nothing in reality, not a single dime of it is mine. You may ask, Do you feel as you say? Yes, I actually do. The coat I have on my back is not mine, and never was; the Lord put it in my possession honorably, and I wear it; but if he wishes for it, and all there is under it, he is welcome to the whole. I do not own a house, or a single farm of land, a horse, mule, carriage, or wagon, or wife, nor child, but what the Lord gave me, and if he wants them, he can take them at his pleasure, whether he speaks for them, or takes them without speaking. (*Journal of Discourses* 2:307.)

When I cast my eyes upon the inhabitants of the earth and see the weakness, and I may say, the height of folly in the hearts of the kings, rulers, and the great, and those who should be wise and good and noble; when I see them groveling in the dust; longing, craving, desiring, contending for the things of this life, I think, O foolish men, to set your hearts on the things of this life! Today they are seeking after the honors and glories of the world, and by the time the sun is hidden by the western mountains the breath is gone out of their nostrils, they sink to their mother earth. Where are their riches then? Gone forever. As Job says, Naked I came into the world. Destitute and forlorn, they have to travel a path that is untried and unknown to them, and wend their way into the spirit world. They know not where they are going nor for what. The designs of the Creator are hidden from their eyes; darkness, ignorance, mourning and groaning take hold of them and they pass into eternity. And this is the end of them concerning this life as far as they know.

A man or a woman who places the wealth of this world and the things of time in the scales against the things of God and the wisdom of eternity, has no eyes to see, no ears to hear, no heart to understand. What are riches for? For blessings, to do good. Then let us dispense that which the Lord gives us to the best possible use for the building up of his Kingdom, for the promotion of the truth on the earth, that we may see and enjoy the blessings of the Zion of God here upon this earth.

I look around among the world of mankind and see them grabbing, scrambling, contending, and every one seeking to

aggrandize himself, and to accomplish his own individual purposes, passing the community by, walking upon the heads of his
neighbors—all are seeking, planning, contriving in their wakeful
hours, and when asleep dreaming, How can I get the advantage of
my neighbor? How can I spoil him, that I may ascend the ladder
of fame? This is entirely a mistaken idea. You see that nobleman
seeking the benefit of all around him, trying to bring, we will
say, his servants, if you please, his tenants, to his knowledge,
to like blessings, that he enjoys, to dispense his wisdom and
talent among them and to make them equal with himself. As they
ascend and increase, so does he, and he is in the advance. All
eyes are upon that king or that nobleman, and the feelings of
those around him are, God bless him! How I love him! How I
delight in him! He seeks to bless and to fill me with joy, to crown
my labors with success, to give me comfort, that I may enjoy the
world as well as himself. But the man who seeks honor and glory
at the expense of his fellow-men is not worthy of the society of
the intelligent. (*Journal of Discourses* 15:18.)

When they bow down to worship the Lord, they acknowledge
that the earth is his, and the cattle upon a thousand hills; and
tell the Lord there is no sacrifice they are not willing to make for
the sake of the religion of Jesus Christ. The people were crying
this continually among the churches when the Book of Mormon
came forth, and the Lord spoke through Joseph, revealing the
law of consecration, to see whether they were willing to do as
they said in their prayers. (*Journal of Discourses* 2:305.)

When men are Saints, they will bring their thousands and lay
them at the feet of the Bishops, Apostles, and Prophets, saying,
Here is my money; it is now where it should be. (*Journal of
Discourses* 6:175.)

When the Lord gave the revelation instructing us in our duty
as to consecrating what we have, if the people then could have
understood things precisely as they are, and had obeyed that

revelation, it would have been neither more nor less than yielding up that which is not their own, to him to whom it belongs. And so it is now. (*Journal of Discourses* 2:303.)

Debt

Be prompt in everything, and especially to pay your debts. (*Journal of Discourses* 14:279.)

A man who will not pay his honest debts is no Latter-day Saint, if he has the means to pay them. (*Journal of Discourses* 11:258.)

A man who will run into debt, when he has no prospect of paying it back again, does not understand the principles that should prevail in a well regulated community, or he is willfully dishonest. (*Journal of Discourses* 13:258.)

It is bad enough, quite bad enough, to borrow from an enemy and not to repay him; to do this is beneath the character of any human being; but all who will borrow from a friend, and especially from the poor, are undeserving the fellowship of the Saints if they do not repay. (*Journal of Discourses* 14:276.)

Tithing

If the Lord requires one-tenth of my ability to be devoted to building temples, meeting houses, schoolhouses, to schooling our children, gathering the poor from the nations of the earth, bringing home the aged, lame, halt and blind, and building houses for them to live in, that they may be comfortable when they reach Zion, and to sustaining the Priesthood, it is not my prerogative to question the authority of the Almighty in this, nor of his servants who have charge of it. If I am required to pay my tithing it is my duty to pay it. In the days of Joseph, when my circumstances were very, very straitened, I never had 500, 100, one dollar, fifty cents or twenty-five cents, but what, if it were wanted, it went as free as a cup of water from a well—Joseph was welcome to it. Was I tried in this? Yes, for many and many has been the time in my poverty, when if I had a dollar or fifty cents in my possession I have thought, I can buy a pint or a half pint of molasses for my children to sop their bread in, but it was called for, and it went as free as the water of the river here would be to a thirsty person. And as for my time, from the day that I entered this Church until now, I have paid no attention to any business except that of building up this Kingdom. The question may be asked, Do you not attend to your private affairs and business? Yes, when I can, but I do not know that I have ever spent one minute in attending to business belonging to Brigham Young, when the business of the Church and Kingdom of God on the earth required his attention. Yet I would not say that this is any excuse for not strictly paying my tithing. I have paid a great deal of tithing, more perhaps than any other man, or any other ten men who were ever in the Church, and yet my tithing is not paid. But I pay tithing, and when the grain upon my farm is ripened, or the cattle upon it are matured, I say to my men, Be sure and pay the tithing on whatever we have raised. But in some instances I have found that it was neglected. (*Journal of Discourses* 16:111.)

If we live our religion we will be willing to pay tithing. (*Journal of Discourses* 10:283.)

In regard to this whining of the world about Brigham's handling the tithing, I can say that he has put in ten dollars where he has taken one out of the treasury, and he has paid more tithing than any other man in the Church. Everybody should pay their tenth. A poor woman ought to pay her tenth chicken, if she has to draw out ten times its value for her support. It is all the Lord's and we are only his stewards. (*Journal of Discourses* 16:45.)

It is my business to control the disbursements of the tithing paid by the Saints, and not the business of every Elder in the

Kingdom who thinks the tithing belongs to him. (*Journal of Discourses* 8:170.)

It is very true that the poor pay their tithing better than the rich do. If the rich would pay their tithing we should have plenty. The poor are faithful and prompt in paying their tithing, but the rich can hardly afford to pay theirs—they have too much. If he has only ten dollars he can pay one; if he has only one dollar he can pay ten cents; it does not hurt him at all. If he has a hundred dollars he can possibly pay ten. If he has a thousand dollars he looks over it a little and says, I guess I will pay it; it ought to be paid anyhow; and he manages to pay his ten dollars or his hundred dollars. But suppose a man is wealthy enough to pay ten thousand, he looks that over a good many times and says, I guess I will wait until I get a little more, and then I will pay a good deal. And they wait and wait, like an old gentleman in the East; he waited and waited and waited to pay his tithing until he went out of the world, and this is the way with a great many. They wait and continue waiting, until, finally, the character comes along who is called Death, and he slips up to them and takes away their breath, then they are gone and cannot pay their tithing, they are too late, and so it goes. (*Journal of Discourses* 15:163–164.)

It may be supposed by some that the tithing is used to sustain and feed the First Presidency and the Twelve; this is a false impression. I can say, without boasting, that there is not another man in this Kingdom has done more in dollars and cents to build it up than I have, and yet I have not done a farthing's worth of myself, for the means I have handled God has given me; it is not mine, and if it ever is mine it will be when I have overcome and gained my exaltation and received it from him who rightfully owns all things. (*Journal of Discourses* 10:270.)

One thing is required at the hands of this people, and to understand which there is no necessity for receiving a commandment every year, viz.: to pay their tithing. I do not suppose for a moment, that there is a person in this Church, who is unacquainted with the duty of paying tithing, neither is it necessary to have revelation every year upon the subject. There is the Law—pay one-tenth. (*Journal of Discourses* 1:278.)

Pay your tithing, just because you like to, not unless you want to. They say we cut people off the Church for not paying tithing; we never have yet, but they ought to be. God does not fellowship them. The law of tithing is an eternal law. The Lord Almighty never had his Kingdom on the earth without the law of tithing being in the midst of his people, and he never will. It is an eternal law that God has instituted for the benefit of the human family, for their salvation and exaltation. This law is in the Priesthood, but we do not want any to observe it unless they are willing to do so. (*Journal of Discourses* 14:89.)

Some complain and say that they are taxed by tithing. We ask no tithing of any man. In this we are as independent as the Lord is. I say, do not pay another dollar in tithing unless you want to. (*Journal of Discourses* 8:345.)

The little moiety that is now paid on tithing is used to bring the poor here, to find them houses to live in, bread to eat, and wood to burn. Now, suppose we had a little more of this surplus on hand, could we not help the brethren on their way to preach the Gospel to the nations? Yes, we could. Some of them will leave families that will, probably, be destitute, and if we had means on hand we could donate to help them, and to prevent them from running continually to the Bishops. (*Journal of Discourses* 12:36.)

The Lord instituted tithing; it was practiced in the days of Abraham, and Enoch and Adam and his children did not forget their tithes and offerings. You can read for yourselves with regard to what the Lord requires. I want to say this much to those who profess to be Latter-day Saints—if we neglect our tithes and offerings we will receive the chastening hand of the Lord. We may just as well count on this first as last. If we neglect to pay our tithes and offerings we will neglect other things and this will grow upon us until the spirit of the Gospel is entirely gone from us, and we are in the dark, and know not whither we are going. (*Journal of Discourses* 15:163.)

The Lord requires one-tenth of that which he has given me; it is for me to pay the one-tenth of the increase of my flocks and of all that I have, and all the people should do the same. The question may arise, What is to be done with the tithing? It is for the building of temples to God; for the enlarging of the borders of Zion; sending Elders on missions to preach the Gospel and taking care of their families. By and by we shall have some temples to go into, and we will receive our blessings, the blessings of heaven, by obedience to the doctrine of tithing. We shall have temples built throughout these mountains, in the valleys of this Territory and the valleys of the next Territory, and finally, all through these mountain valleys. We expect to build temples in a great many valleys. We go to the Endowment House, and before going, we get a recommendation from our Bishop that we have paid our tithing. (*Journal of Discourses* 16:168.)

The Lord's poor do not forget their covenants, while the Devil's poor pay no regard to their promises. (*Journal of Discourses* 3:2.)

The people are not compelled to pay their tithing, they do as they please about it, it is urged upon them only as a matter of duty between them and their God. (*Journal of Discourses* 12:36.)

We are not our own, we are bought with a price, we are the Lord's; our time, our talents, our gold and silver, our wheat and fine flour, our wine and our oil, our cattle, and all there is on this earth that we have in our possession is the Lord's, and he requires one-tenth of this for the building up of his Kingdom. Whether we have much or little, one-tenth should be paid in for tithing. (*Journal of Discourses* 14:88.)

We do not ask anybody to pay tithing, unless they are disposed to do so; but if you pretend to pay tithing, pay it like honest men. (*Journal of Discourses* 8:202.)

What object have I in saying to the Latter-day Saints, do this, that or the other? It is for my own benefit, it is for your benefit; it is for my own wealth and happiness, and for your wealth and happiness that we pay tithing and render obedience to any requirement of Heaven. We can not add anything to the Lord by doing these things. Tell about making sacrifices for the Kingdom of heaven. There is no man who ever made a sacrifice on this earth for the Kingdom of heaven, that I know anything about, except the Savior. He drank the bitter cup to the dregs, and tasted for every man and for every woman, and redeemed the earth and all things upon it. But he was God in the flesh, or he could not have endured it. But we suffer, we sacrifice, we give something, we have preached so long. What for? Why, for the Lord. I would not give the ashes of a rye straw for the man who feels that he is making sacrifice for God. We are doing this for our own happiness, welfare and exaltation, and for nobody else's. This is the fact, and what we do, we do for the salvation of the inhabitants of the earth, not for the salvation of the heavens, the angels, or the Gods. (*Journal of Discourses* 16:114.)

When my Bishop came to value my property, he wanted to know what he should take my tithing in. I told him to take anything I had, for I did not set my heart upon any one thing; my horses, cows, hogs, or any other thing he might take; my heart is set upon the work of my God, upon the public good of his great Kingdom. (*Journal of Discourses* 1:376.)

Caring for the Poor

A certain portion of the human family have to be looked after and taken care of. (*Journal of Discourses* 11:328.)

Before you preach to a starving man to arise and be baptized, first carry him some bread and wine; first unlock his prison house and let him go free. (*Journal of Discourses,* 10:33.)

Do not oppress the poor, but trust in God, and you will go neither hungry, naked, nor thirsty. If you oppress the poor, the day will come when you will be naked, thirsty, and hungry, and will not be able to get anything to supply your wants. (*Journal of Discourses* 8:73.)

The customs of the world have made it degrading to ask for food, but it is not, when a person cannot honestly procure it in any other way. The man who is hungry and destitute has as good a right to my food as any other person, and I should feel as happy in associating with him, if he had a good heart, as with those who have an abundance, or with the princes of the earth. They all are esteemed by me, not according to the wealth and position they hold, but according to the character they have. (*Journal of Discourses* 3:245.)

If a man comes to me and says he is out of food, what of that? He is out of food; that is all. If a man comes along and says, My family is destitute of food and clothing, what of that? Simply that they are destitute of food and clothing, and still they may be gentlemen and ladies, for all that, and be honoring their tabernacles and being on the earth.

We have not in our society an aristocratic circle. Whether a brother wears a coon skin cap or a fine beaver hat is all the same to us. If a person is a faithful servant of God we do not object to his coming to meeting, though he has only a piece of buffalo skin to wear on his head. We partake of the Sacrament with him, hail him in the street as a brother and a friend, converse with him, meet him in social parties and greet him as an equal. (*Journal of Discourses* 9:188.)

If you come naked and barefooted (I would not care if you had naught but a deer skin around you when you arrive here), and bring your God and your religion, you are a thousand times better than if you come with wagonloads of silver and gold and left your God behind. (*Journal of Discourses* 4:204.)

The first year that I came into this valley I had not flour enough to last my family until harvest, and that I had brought with me, and persons were coming to my house every day for bread. I had the blues about it one day; I went down to the old fort, and by the time I got back to my house I was completely cured. I said to my wife, "Do not let a person come here for food and go away empty-handed, for if you do we shall suffer before harvest; but if you give to every individual that comes we shall have enough to last us through." (*Journal of Discourses,* 3:332–33.)

It is a disgrace to every man and woman that has sense enough to live, not to take care of their own relatives, their own poor, and plan for them to do something they are able to do. (*Journal of Discourses* 8:145.)

We have among us some brethren and sisters who are not strong, nor healthy, and they must be supported. We wish to adopt the most economical plan of taking care of them, and we say to you Bishops, take care of them. (*Journal of Discourses* 12:114.)

True charity to a poor family or person consists of placing them in a situation in which they can support themselves. (*Messages of the First Presidency,* 2:134.)

If you see any young, middle-aged or old ladies in need find them something to do that will enable them to sustain themselves; but don't relieve the idle, for relieving those who are able but unwilling to work is ruinous to any community. (*Journal of Discourses* 14:107.)

My experience has taught me, and it has become a principle with me, that it is never any benefit to give, out and out, to man or woman, money, food, clothing, or anything else, if they are able-bodied, and can work and earn what they need, when there is anything on the earth for them to do. This is my principle, and I try to act upon it. To pursue a contrary course would ruin any community in the world and make them idlers. (*Journal of Discourses* 11:297.)

Let the poor, those who have to depend upon their brethren for bread, after they have done all they can to obtain it themselves, be thankful, and take no more than they require to use in a frugal manner. (*Journal of Discourses* 3:375.)

A great many good men would say to me "Br. Brigham, you have a gold ring on your finger, why not give it to the poor?" Because to do so would make them worse off. Go to work and get a gold ring, then you will have yours and I will have mine. (*Journal of Discourses* 12:61.)

You who are poor and want me to sell that ring, go to work and I will dictate you how to make yourselves comfortable, and how to adorn your bodies and become delightful. But no, in many instances you would say—"We will not have your counsel, we want your money and your property." This is not what the Lord wants of us. (*Journal of Discourses* 12:61.)

Instead of saying that I shall give up my carriage for the poor to ride in, we will direct the poor so that every man may have his carriage, if he will be obedient to the requirements of the Almighty. (*Journal of Discourses* 17:53.)

Says one, "It was preached thirty years ago, that nothing belongs to us, and, if I have a thousand dollars, to at once give it all to the poor." That is your enthusiasm and ignorance. (*Journal of Discourses* 4:29.)

How could you ever get a people equal with regard to their possessions? They never can be, no more than they can be in the appearance of their faces. (*Journal of Discourses* 4:29.)

The poor are filled with idolatry as well as the rich, and covet the means of those who have helped them; the rich also have the same spirit of idolatry, and stick to what they have. Let the poor be honest, let the rich be liberal, and lay their plans to assist the poor, to build up the Kingdom of God, and at the same time enrich themselves, for that is the way to build up God's Kingdom. (*Journal of Discourses* 3:6.)

You take these very characters who are so anxious for the poor, and what would they tell us? Just what they told us back yonder— "Sell your feather beds, your gold rings, ear rings, breast pins, necklaces, your silver tea spoons or table spoons, or anything valuable that you have in the world, to help the poor." I recollect once the people wanted to sell their jewellery to help the poor; I told them that would not help them. The people wanted to sell such things so that they might be able to bring into camp three, ten, or a hundred bushels of com meal. Then they would sit down and eat it up, and they would have nothing with which to buy another hundred bushels of meal, and would be just where they started. My advice was for them to keep their jewellery and valuables, and to set the poor to work—setting out orchards, splitting rails, digging ditches, making fences, or anything useful, and so enable them to buy meal and flour and the necessaries of life. (*Journal of Discourses* 12:60-61.)

Were you to make an equal distribution of property today, one year would not pass before there would be as great an inequality as now. How could you ever get a people equal with regard to their possessions? They never can be, no more than they can be in the appearance of their faces. (*Journal of Discourses* 4:29.)

Poor men, or poor women, who have nothing, and covet that which is not their own, are just as wicked in their hearts, as the miserly man who hoards up his gold and silver, and will not put it out to use. I wish the poor to understand, and act as they would wish others to act towards them in like circumstances. (*Journal of Discourses* 2:52.)

If the poor had all the surplus property of the rich many of them would waste it on the lusts of the flesh, and destroy themselves in using it. For this reason the Lord does not require the rich to give all their substance to the poor. It is true that when the young man came to Jesus to know what he must do to be saved, he told him, finally, sell all that thou hast and distribute unto the poor, and thou shalt have treasure in heaven, and come, follow me; and a great many think that he told the young man to give away all that he had, but Jesus did not require any such thing, neither did he say so, but simply, distribute to the poor. If the poor knew what to do with what they have many, yea very many, in this land would have all that is necessary to make them comfortable. (*Journal of Discourses* 13:302.)

If they had the privilege of dictating the affairs of this people, or of any other, they would divide the substance of the rich among the poor, and make all what they call equal. But the question would arise with me at once, how long would they remain equal? Make the rich and the poor of this community, or of any other, equal by the distribution of their earthly substance, and how long would it be before a certain portion of them would be calling upon the other portion, for something with which to sustain themselves? The cry would soon be—I have no bread, no house, no team, no farm; I have nothing. And in a very few years, at the most, large properties would thus pass from the hands of such individuals, and would be distributed among those who know how to accumulate wealth and to preserve it when accumulated. (*Journal of Discourses* 12:56.)

You take these very men and women who want to make us all equal, and they tell us that we are covetous, because we have horses, carriages, houses, lands, and money. Have the poor got greedy eyes? Are they covetous and penurious? I shall go a little too far if I am not careful. I must guard myself, because the Lord has chosen the poor of this world. But what kind of poor? Now the poor may be divided into three classes. In the first place there is the Lord's poor, of which you may pick up one here and another there, one in a city, two in a family. Is there any other kind? Yes, you come across a certain class that may be called the Devil's poor. Is there any other class? Yes, there is another class, who, long before I ever mentioned them, were denominated poor devils. Hence we have the Lord's poor, the devil's poor, and poor devils. (*Journal of Discourses* 12:57.)

The poor are the people of God, and they shall inherit the earth. (*Journal of Discourses* 8:186.)

If I had only seen in my young days an interest manifested by those who had wealth, power and influence to reach down a hand to take the suffering, ignorant poor and elevate them to the standard they occupied, and to place them in possession of every comfort, it would have been a matter of great joy to me. But it was not so then, neither is it now. Men generally use their wealth for selfish purposes, and do not seek to devote it to God and to the glory of his name. (*Journal of Discourses* 13:147.)

Here is a character—a man—that God has created, organized, fashioned and made,—every part and particle of my system from the top of my head to the soles of my feet, has been produced by my Father in Heaven; and he requires one-tenth part of my brain, heart, nerve, muscle, sinew, flesh, bone, and of my whole system, for the building of temples, for the ministry, for sustaining missionaries and missionaries' families, for feeding the poor, the aged, the halt and blind, and for gathering them home from the nations and taking care of them after they are gathered. He has said, My son, devote one-tenth of yourself to the good and wholesome work of taking care of your fellow-beings, preaching the Gospel, bringing people into the Kingdom; lay your plans to take care of those who cannot take care of themselves; direct the labors of those who are able to labor; and one-tenth part is all-sufficient if it is devoted properly, carefully and judiciously for the advancement of my Kingdom on the earth. (*Journal of Discourses* 16:69.)

You count me out fifty, a hundred, five hundred, or a thousand of the poorest men and women you can find in this community; with the means that I have in my possession, I will take these ten, fifty, hundred, five hundred, or a thousand people, and put them to labor; but only enough to benefit their health and to make their food and sleep sweet unto them, and in ten years I will make that community wealthy. In ten years I will put six, a hundred, or a thousand individuals, whom we have to support now by donations, in a position not only to support themselves, but they shall be wealthy, shall ride in their carriages, have fine houses to live in, orchards to go to, flocks and herds and everything to make them comfortable. (*Journal of Discourses* 14:88.)

If we would work together in our farming, in our mechanism, be obedient and work as a family for the good of all, it would be almost impossible for anybody to guess the success we would have. But we have got to do it in the Lord. We must not do it with a covetous heart. Always be ready and willing that the Lord should have it all, and do what he pleases with it. I have asked a favor of the Lord in this thing, and that is not to place me in such circumstances that what He has given me shall go into the hands of our enemies. God forbid that! But let it go for the preaching of the Gospel, to sustain and to gather the poor, to build factories, make farms, and set the poor to work, as I have hundreds and thousands that had not anything to do. I have fed and clothed them and taken care of them until they have become comparatively independent. I have made no man poor, but thousands and thousands rich, that is, the Lord has, through your humble servant. (*Journal of Discourses* 15:166.)

My plan and counsel would be, let every person, able to work,

work and earn what he needs; and if the poor come around me—able-bodied men and women—take them and put them into the house. (*Journal of Discourses* 11:297.)

What causes poverty among this people? It is the want of discretion, calculation, sound judgment. I am paying men more or less by the day, and where do you see those who get the least wages? Seated back in the barber's chair three or four times a week. Next at a store to get a box of blacking to put upon fifteen dollar boots, if they can get them. They must have four or five dollar handkerchiefs, as fine things for their wives and children, and as much in quantity as any other man has. At the end of the year there are two or three hundred dollars on the debit side of their accounts. (*Journal of Discourses* 9:297.)

There are many in the city of New York who never went to school a day in their lives; they are wallowing in the gutter, ragged, dirty, and filthy. They learn sharpness, it is true; but where do they sleep? By the wayside, or crawl into some old building—girls and boys, and live there by the thousand. They have not a shelter to place their heads under, but when night comes their only refuge is old buildings, hovels, and corners of streets forsaken by the police, and there they must spend the night. Why not take such characters and bring them out to this country, or to California, Oregon, or to the plains of Illinois, Wisconsin, etc., and make a town, settle up the country, and make these poor, miserable creatures better off? You would prove yourselves worthy of existence on the earth if you would. (*Journal of Discourses* 14:84.)

The Gospel of life and salvation does not reduce those who obey it to beggary; but it takes the poor and the ignorant, makes them wise and happy, and surrounds them with the comforts of life and everything desirable, and teaches them to serve God with all their hearts. (*Journal of Discourses* 14:121.)

Now the object is to improve the minds of the inhabitants of the earth, until we learn what we are here for, and become one before the Lord, that we may rejoice together and be equal. Not to make all poor, no. The whole world is before us. The earth is here, and the fulness thereof is here. It was made for man; and one man was not made to trample his fellow man under his feet, and enjoy all his heart desires, while the thousands suffer. We will take a moral view, a political view, and we see the inequality that exists in the human family. We take the inhabitants of the civilized world, and how many laboring men are there in proportion to the inhabitants? About one to every five that are producers, and the supposition is that ten hours, work by the one to three persons in the twenty-four hours will support the five. It is an unequal condition to mankind.

We see servants that labor early and late, and that have not the opportunity of measuring their hours ten in twenty-four. They cannot go to school, nor hardly get clothing to go to meeting in on the Sabbath. I have seen many cases of this kind in Europe, when the young lady would have to take her clothing on a Saturday night and wash it, in order that she might go to meeting on the Sunday with a clean dress on. Who is she laboring for? For those who, many of them, are living in luxury. And, to serve the classes that are living on them, the poor, laboring men and women are toiling, working their lives out to earn that which will keep a little life within them. Is this equality? No. What is going to be done? The Latter-day Saints will never accomplish their mission until this inequality shall cease on the earth. (*Journal of Discourses* 19:46.)

Unity and Cooperation

I have looked upon the community of Latter-day Saints in vision and beheld them organized as one great family of heaven, each person performing his several duties in his line of industry, working for the good of the whole more than for individual aggrandizement; and in this I have beheld the most beautiful order that the mind of man can contemplate, and the grandest results for the upbuilding of the Kingdom of God and the spread of righteousness upon the earth. Will this people ever come to this order of things? Are they now prepared to live according to that patriarchal order that will be organized among the true and faithful before God receives his own? We all concede the point that when this mortality falls off, and with it its cares, anxieties, love of self, love of wealth, and love of power, and all the conflicting interests which pertain to this flesh, that then, when our spirits have returned to God who gave them, we will be subject to every requirement that he may make of us, that we shall then live together as one great family; our interest will be a general, a common interest. Why can we not so live in this world? (*Journal of Discourses* 12:153.)

Jesus offered up one of the most essential prayers that could possibly be offered up by a human or heavenly being—no matter who, pertaining to the salvation of the people, and embodying a principle without which none can be saved, when he prayed the Father to make His disciples one, as He and His Father were one. He knew that if they did not become one, they could not be saved in the celestial Kingdom of God. If persons do not see as he did while in the flesh, hear as he heard, understand as he understood, and become precisely as he was, according to their several capacities and callings, they can never dwell with Him and His Father. (*Journal of Discourses* 6:96.)

If we were one, we should then prove to heaven, to God our Father, to Jesus Christ our Elder Brother, to the angels, to the good upon the earth, and to all mankind that we are the disciples of the lord Jesus Christ. If we are not one, we are not in the true sense of the word the disciples of the Lord Jesus. (*Journal of Discourses* 11:273.)

If we will live so that Christ can make us one through our obedience, where are wars and contentions? All will cease. Where is the spirit of bickering? There will be no more of it. (*Journal of Discourses* 14:209.)

Would you like to live at ease and get rich? Would you like to keep your homes in this city? I know you would. You can do so by being one in all things. (*Journal of Discourses* 11:278.)

If we will work unitedly, we can work ourselves into wealth, health, prosperity and power, and this is required of us. It is the duty of a Saint of God to gain all the influence he can on this earth, and to use every particle of that influence to do good. If this is not his duty, I do not understand what the duty of man is. (*Journal of Discourses* 12:376.)

You will find that if the people unitedly hearken to the counsel that is given them, it will not be long before the hats, caps, bonnets, boots and shoes, pants, coats, vests and underclothing of this entire community will all be made in our midst. (*Journal of Discourses* 13:3.)

Implied faith and confidence in God is for you and me to do everything we can to sustain and preserve ourselves; and the community that works together, heart and hand, to accomplish this, their efforts will be like the efforts of one man. (*Journal of Discourses* 4:25.)

I want you to be united. If we should build up and organize a community, we would have to do it on the principle of oneness, it is one of the simplest things I know of. A city of one hundred thousand or a million of people could be united into a perfect family, and they would work together as beautifully as the different parts of the carding machine work together. Why, we could organize millions into a family under the Order of Enoch. (*Journal of Discourses* 16:170.)

We have been gathered from many nations, and speak many languages; we have been ruled by different nationalities, and educated in different religions, yet we dwell together in Utah under one government, believe in the same God and worship Him in the same way, and we are all one in Christ Jesus. The world wonder at this, and fear the union that prevails among this, as they are called, singular people. Why is this? It is because the Spirit of the Lord Almighty is in the people, and they follow its dictates, and they hearken to the truth, and live by it; this unites them in one, and causeth them to dwell together in peace. (*Journal of Discourses* 11:124.)

When truth comes, receive it as from the Lord, and let everything be simplified to us as unto children, for the Lord has ordained that we may grow in grace, and in the knowledge of the truth, and be able to receive more knowledge, wisdom, and understanding, and it is not possible for us to receive it any other way, only as we apply our hearts strictly to overcome every evil and cleave to that which is pleasing to the Lord—to that which tends to life and salvation. This is the only channel in which we can become of one heart, and of one mind. (*Journal of Discourses* 3:355.)

Will the time ever come that we can commence and organize this people as a family? It will. Do we know how? Yes; what was lacking in these revelations from Joseph to enable us to do so was revealed to me. Do you think we will ever be one? When we get home to our Father and God, will we not wish to be in the family? Will it not be our highest ambition and desire to be reckoned as the sons of the living God, as the daughters of the Almighty, with a right to the household, and the faith that belongs to the household, heirs of the Father, his goods, his wealth, his power, his excellency, his knowledge and wisdom? (*Journal of Discourses* 11:326.)

We must become of one heart and mind, in order to fully enjoy the blessings we anticipate. (*Journal of Discourses* 6:41.)

We never shall become one to that extent that we shall look alike or possess precisely the same mental power and ability; this is not the design of heaven. But we expect to become one in all our operations to bring for the fulness of the Kingdom of God on the earth, that Jesus may come and reign King of nations as He does King of Saints. Shall we call this a union for political purposes? I say it is good policy for people to be of one heart and mind in all their operations. (*Journal of Discourses* 12:35.)

We should be one, there is no doubt of that, but the very men and women who would take the property of the rich and dispose of it to their own advantage, would spurn from their presence and disregard every word of counsel given by those who know how to accumulate and preserve, and they would say, "We know as much as you, and we can dictate our own affairs." So they can, until they make themselves poor and have to be helped by others. (*Journal of Discourses* 12:56.)

The Lord Almighty has not the least objection in the world to our entering into the Order of Enoch. I will stand between the people and all harm in this. He has not the least objection to any man, every man, all mankind on the face of the earth turning from evil and loving and serving him with all their hearts. With regard to all those orders that the Lord has revealed, it depends upon the will and doings of the people, and we are at liberty from this Conference, to go and build up a settlement, or we can join ourselves together in this city, do it legally—according to the laws of the land—and enter into covenant with each other by a firm agreement that we will live as a family, that we will put our property into the hands of a committee of trustees, who shall dictate the affairs of this society. (*Journal of Discourses* 16:8.)

The Lord has declared it to be his will that his people enter into covenant, even as Enoch and his people did, which of necessity must be before we shall have the privilege of building the Center Stake of Zion, for the power and glory of God will be there, and none but the pure in heart will be able to live and enjoy it. (*Journal of Discourses* 18:263.)

Suppose there was a union of effort in every political and financial matter undertaken for the benefit of the whole people, who cannot see the good that would result? We have tried this to some extent in relation to our markets here; but suppose we were fully agreed on the point, we could demand a fair price for our products, and we need not be imposed upon by traders and traffickers. If we were agreed we could supply ourselves from distant markets, say with our clothing, at a far less cost than now. (*Journal of Discourses* 12:35.)

That perfect union, which must ultimately be enjoyed by the Latter-day Saints, can only be brought about by every man and woman living so as to keep their minds pure and unspotted like a piece of clean, white paper, being constantly free from the love of the world, that the spirit of revelation may easily indite upon the heart whatever is the mind and will of the Lord. We cannot be truly the members of Christ's mystical body without living in this way, that the Spirit may indite as easily upon the heart the things of God, as these brethren, our reporters can write with ink on paper. (*Journal of Discourses* 11:19.)

Now, besides being our duty to pray, it is our duty to live in peace with one another. It is also our duty to love the Gospel and the spirit of the Gospel, so that we can become one in the Lord, not out of Him, that our faith, our affections for truth, the kingdom of heaven, our acts, all our labor will be concentrated in the salvation of the children of men, and the establishment of the Kingdom of God on the earth. This is co-operation on a very large scale. This is the work of redemption that is entered into by the Latter-day Saints. Unitedly we perform these duties, we stand, we endure, we increase and multiply, we strengthen and spread abroad, and shall continue so to do until the kingdoms of this world are the kingdoms of our God and His Christ. (*Journal of Discourses* 15:63.)

My spiritual enjoyment must be obtained by my own life, but it would add much to the comfort of the community, and to my happiness, as one with them, if every man and woman would live their religion, and enjoy the light and glory of the Gospel for themselves, be passive, humble and faithful; rejoice continually before the Lord, attend to the business they are called to do, and be sure never to do anything wrong. (*Discourses of Brigham Young,* 119.)

Shall we ever see the time we shall be perfectly independent of every other being in all the eternities? No; we shall never see that time. Many have fallen on as simple ground as this. . . . Such persons think they have power to do this, that, and the other, but they are left to themselves, and the Lord loves to show them they have no power. (*Discourses of Brigham Young,* 426.)

The Church of Jesus Christ could not exist, and be divided up into parties. Where such disunion exists in any government, it ultimately becomes the means of the utter overthrow of that government or people, unless a timely remedy is applied. Party spirit once made its appearance in heaven, but was promptly checked. (*Journal of Discourses* 9:332.)

The closer the connection in a business point of view that a community hold themselves together, the greater will be their joy and wealth. I am prepared to prove, from all the facts that have existed or that now exist in all branches of human affairs, that union is strength, and that division is weakness and confusion. (*Journal of Discourses* 13:267.)

The religion of heaven unites the hearts of the people and makes them one. You may gather a people together, and no matter how widely they differ in politics, the Gospel of Jesus Christ will make them one, even if among them were found members of all the political parties in the country. If members of all these various organizations were to obey the Gospel and gather together, the religion of heaven would clear their hearts of all political rubbish and make them one in voting for principles and measures, instead of men, and I think that any religion that will not do this is very feeble in its effects. (*Journal of Discourses* 14:159.)

The Savior sought continually to impress upon the minds of His disciples that a perfect oneness reigned among all celestial beings—that the Father and the Son and their Minister, the Holy Ghost, were one in their administration in heaven and among the people pertaining to this earth. Between them and all the heavenly hosts there can be no disunion, no discord, no wavering on a suggestion, on a thought or reflection, on a feeling or manifestation; for such a principle would differ widely from the character of him who dictates them, who makes his throne the habitation of justice, mercy, equity, and truth. If the heavenly hosts were not one, they would be entirely unfit to dwell in the eternal burnings with the Father and Ruler of the universe. (*Journal of Discourses* 7:276.)

If we are united, we are independent of the powers of hell and of the world. (*Journal of Discourses* 5:257.)

Except I am one with my good brethren, do not say that I am a Latter-day Saint. We must be one. Our faith must be concentrated in one great work—the building up of the Kingdom of God on the earth, and our works must aim at the accomplishment of that great purpose. (*Journal of Discourses* 7:280.)

I can see no good accruing to this community in maintaining a divided interest; our interest must be one throughout, in order to produce the good we desire.

I pray, my brethren, the Bishops, the Elders, the Seventies, the Apostles, yea, every man and woman and child who has named the name of Christ, to be of one heart and of one mind, for if we do not become of one heart and mind we shall surely perish by the way. (*Journal of Discourses* 12:156.)

A perfect oneness will save a people, because intelligent beings cannot become perfectly one, only by acting upon principles that pertain to eternal life. Wicked men may be partially united in evil; but, in the very nature of things, such a union is of short duration. The very principle upon which they are partially united will itself breed contention and disunion to destroy the temporary compact. Only the line of truth and righteousness can secure to any kingdom or people, either of earthly or heavenly existence, an eternal continuation of perfect union; for only truth and those who are sanctified by it can dwell in celestial glory. (*Journal of Discourses* 7:277.)

I know how to start such a society, right in this city, and how to make its members rich. I would go to now, and buy out the poorest Ward in this city, and then commence with men and women who have not a dollar in the world. Bring them here from England, or any part of the earth, set them down in this Ward and put them to work, and in five years we would begin to enter other Wards, and we would buy this house and that house, and the next house, and we would add Ward to Ward until we owned the whole city, every dollar's worth of property there is in it. We could do this, and let the rich go to California to get gold, and we would buy their property. Would you like to know how to do this? I can tell you in a very few words—never want a thing you cannot get, live within your means, manufacture that which you wear, and raise that which you eat. Raise every calf and lamb; raise the chickens, and have your eggs, make your butter and cheese, and always have a little to spare. The first year we raise a crop, and we have more than we want. We buy nothing, we sell a little. The next year we raise more; we buy nothing and we sell more. In this way we could pile up the gold and silver and in twenty years a hundred families working like this could buy out their neighbors. I see men who earn four, five, ten or fifteen dollars a day and spend every dime of it. Such men spend their means foolishly, they waste it instead of taking care of it. They do not know what to do with it, and they seem to fear that it will burn their pockets, and they get rid of it. If you get a dollar, sovereign, half-eagle or eagle, and are afraid it will burn your pockets, put it into a safe. It will not burn anything there, and you will not be forced to spend, spend, spend as you do now. (*Journal of Discourses* 16:11.)

If you will start here and operate together in farming, in making cheese, in herding sheep and cattle and every other kind of work, and get a factory here and co-operative store—I have been told there is no co-operative store here—get a good co-operative store, and operate together in sheep-raising, store-keeping, manufacturing and everything else, no matter what it is, by-and-by, when we can plant ourselves upon a foundation that we cannot be broken up, we shall then proceed to arrange a family organization for which we are not yet quite prepared. You now, right here in this place, commence to carry on your business in a co-operative capacity. In every instance I could show every one of you what a great advantage would be gained in working together; I could reason it out here just how much advantage there is in co-operation in your lumbering and in your herding.

You have men here, I suppose, who have had an arm shot off; they cannot go into the canyons and get out wood. Another, perhaps, has had a leg cut off; he cannot run here and there like some of you; but he can do something; he will make a first-rate shopman, and at keeping books, perhaps, he will be one of the best. He cannot take the scythe and mow; he cannot attend to a threshing machine; he cannot go into the woods lumbering; he could not herd well,—but he could go into the factory, and he can do many things. Well, we can do this and keep up co-operation. I can take fifty men who have not a cent, and if they would do as I would wish them to do, they would soon be worth their thousands, every one of them. (*Journal of Discourses* 16:169.)

Now, I will tell you the facts about this movement. We started the co-operative system here when we thought we would wait no longer; we opened the Wholesale Co-operative Store, and since that, retail stores have been established, although some of the latter were opened before the wholesale store was opened. I know this, that as soon as this movement was commenced the price of goods came down from twenty to thirty percent. I recollect very well, after our vote last October Conference, that it was soon buzzed around, Why, you can get a calico down street at eighteen and seventeen cents a yard; and it came down to sixteen. But when it came down to sixteen cents, who had a chance to buy any? Why, nobody unless it was just a few yards that were sold to them as a favor. But when it came to the Wholesale Co-operative Store the price was put at sixteen cents, and retail stores are selling it today at seventeen and a half or eighteen cents a yard. (*Journal of Discourses* 12:373.)

Let every man and woman be industrious, prudent, and economical in their acts and feelings, and while gathering to themselves, let each one strive to identify his or her interests with the interests of this community, with those of their neighbor and neighborhood, let them seek their happiness and welfare in that of all, and we will be blessed and prospered. (*Journal of Discourses* 3:330.)

When this people become one, it will be one in the Lord. They will not look alike. We will not all have gray, blue, or black eyes. Our features will differ one from another, and in our acts, dispositions, and efforts to accumulate, distribute, and dispose of our time, talents, wealth and whatever the Lord gives to us, in our journey through life, we will differ just as much as in our features. The point that the Lord wishes to bring us to is to obey his counsel and observe his word. Then every one will be dictated so that we can act as a family. (*Journal of Discourses* 12:57.)

Establishing Zion

The purpose of our life should be to build up the Zion of our God, to gather the House of Israel, bring in the fulness of the Gentiles, restore and bless the earth with our ability and make it as the Garden of Eden, store up treasures of knowledge and wisdom in our own understandings, purify our own hearts and prepare a people to meet the Lord when he comes. (*Discourses of Brigham Young*, 88.)

The skill of building up and establishing the Zion of our God on the earth is to take the people and teach them how to take care of themselves. (*Journal of Discourses* 18:354.)

We will have to go to work and get the gold out of the mountains to lay down, if we ever walk in streets paved with gold. The angels that now walk in their golden streets, and they have the tree of life within their paradise, had to obtain that gold and put it there. When we have streets paved with gold, we will have placed it there ourselves. When we enjoy a Zion in its beauty and glory, it will be when we have built it. If we enjoy the Zion that we now anticipate, it will be after we redeem and prepare it. If we live in the city of the New Jerusalem, it will be because we lay the foundation and build it. If we do not as individuals complete that work, we shall lay the foundation for our children and our children's children, as Adam has. If we are to be saved in an ark, as Noah and his family were, it will be because we build it. If the Gospel is preached to the nations, it is because the Elders of Israel in their poverty, without purse or scrip, preach the Gospel to the uttermost parts of the earth. (*Journal of Discourses* 8:354–355.)

The Lord has done his share of the work; he has surrounded us with elements containing wheat, meat, flax, wool, silk, fruit, and everything with which to build up, beautify and glorify the Zion of the last days, and it is our business to mould these elements to our wants and necessities, according to the knowledge we now have and the wisdom we can obtain from the heavens through our faithfulness. In this way will the Lord bring again Zion upon the earth, and in no other. (*Journal of Discourses* 9:283.)

The Lord has blessed me; he has always blessed me; from the time I commenced to build up Zion, I have been extremely blessed. I could relate circumstances of so extraordinary a character in regard to the providences of God to me, that my brethren and sisters would say in their hearts, "I can hardly give credence to this". (*Discourses of Brigham Young*, 452.)

If we are to build up the Kingdom of God, or establish Zion upon the earth, we have to labor with our hands, plan with our minds, and devise ways and means to accomplish that object. (*Journal of Discourses* 3:51.)

Many Latter-day Saints think when they have obeyed the Gospel, made a sacrifice in forsaking their homes, perhaps their parents, husbands, wives, children, farms, native lands, or other things held dear, that the work is done; but it is only just commenced. The work of purifying ourselves and preparing to build up the Zion of God has only just begun with us when we have got as far as that. (*Discourses of Brigham Young*, 444.)

I have Zion in my view constantly. We are not going to wait for angels, or for Enoch and his company to come and build up Zion, but we are going to build it. We will raise our wheat, build our houses, fence our farms, plant our vineyards and orchards, and produce everything that will make our bodies comfortable and happy, and in this manner we intend to build up Zion on the earth and purify it and cleanse it from all pollutions. Let there be an hallowed influence go from us over all things over which we have any power; over the soil we cultivate, over the houses we build, and over everything we possess; and if we cease to hold fellowship with that which is corrupt and establish the Zion of God in our hearts, in our own houses, in our cities, and throughout our country, we shall ultimately overcome the earth, for we are the lords of the earth; and, instead of thorns and

thistles, every useful plant that is good for the food of man and
to beautify and adorn will spring from its bosom. (*Discourses of
Brigham Young*, 443–44.)

Do we realize that if we enjoy a Zion in time or in eternity
we must make it for ourselves? That all, who have a Zion in
the eternities of the Gods, organized, framed, consolidated, and
perfected it themselves, and consequently are entitled to enjoy
it? (*Discourses of Brigham Young*, 118.)

When we conclude to make a Zion we will make it, and this
work commences in the heart of each person. When the father
of a family wishes to make a Zion in his own house, he must
take the lead in this good work, which it is impossible for him
to do unless he himself possesses the spirit of Zion. Before he
can produce the work of sanctification in his family, he must
sanctify himself, and by this means God can help him to sanctify
his family. (*Discourses of Brigham Young*, 118.)

Zion will extend, eventually, all over this earth. There will be
no nook or corner upon the earth but what will be in Zion. It will
all be Zion. (*Discourses of Brigham Young*, 120.)

Everything connected with building up Zion requires actual,
severe labor. It is nonsense to talk about building up any kingdom except by labor; it requires the labor of every part of our
organization, whether it be mental, physical, or spiritual, and
that is the only way to build up the Kingdom of God. (*Journal
of Discourses* 3:122.)

We have been gathered for the express purpose of purifying
ourselves, that we may become polished stones in the temple of
God. We are here for the purpose of establishing the Kingdom
of God on the earth. To be prepared for this work it has been
necessary to gather us out from the nations and countries of the
world [to receive] the ordinances of the holy Priesthood of the
Son of God, which are necessary for the perfection of the Saints
preparatory to his coming. (*Discourses of Brigham Young*, 121.)

We want all the Latter-day Saints to understand how to build up Zion. The City of Zion, in beauty and magnificence, will outstrip anything that is now known upon the earth. The curse will be taken from the earth and sin and corruption will be swept from its face. Who will do this great work? Is the Lord going to convince the people that he will redeem the center Stake of Zion, beautify it and then place them there without an exertion on their part? No. He will not come here to build a Temple, a Tabernacle, a Bowery, or to set out fruit trees, make aprons of fig leaves or coats of skins, or work in brass and iron, for we already know how to do these things. We have to build up Zion, if we do our duty. (*Discourses of Brigham Young,* 120.)

We profess to be Zion. If we are the pure in heart we are so, for "Zion is the pure in heart." Where is Zion? Where the organization of the Church of God is. And may it dwell spiritually in every heart; and may we so live as to enjoy the spirit of Zion always! (*Discourses of Brigham Young,* 118.)

We have come here to build up Zion. How shall we do it? We have got to be united in our efforts. We should go to work with a united faith like the heart of one man; and whatever we do should be performed in the name of the Lord, and we will then be blessed and prospered in all we do. We have a work on hand whose magnitude can hardly be told. (*Discourses of Brigham Young,*284.)

We have no business here other than to build up and establish the Zion of God. It must be done according to the will and law of God, after that pattern and order by which Enoch built up and perfected the former-day Zion, which was taken away to heaven, hence the saying went abroad that Zion had fled. By and by it will come back again, and as Enoch prepared his people to be worthy of translation, so we, through our faithfulness, must prepare ourselves to meet Zion from above when it shall return to earth, and to abide the brightness and glory of its coming. (*Discourses of Brigham Young*, 443.)

We look forward to the day when the Lord will prepare for the building of the New Jerusalem, preparatory to the City of Enoch's going to be joined with it when it is built upon this earth. We are anticipating to enjoy that day, whether we sleep in death previous to that, or not. We look forward, with all the anticipation and confidence that children can possess in a parent, that we shall be there when Jesus comes; and if we are not there, we will come with him: in either case we shall be there when he comes. (*Discourses of Brigham Young*, 120.)

There is not one thing wanting in all the works of God's hands to make a Zion upon the earth when the people conclude to make it. We can make a Zion of God on earth at our pleasure, upon the same principle that we can raise a field of wheat, or build and inhabit. There has been no time when the material has not been here from which to produce corn, wheat, etc, and by the judicious management and arrangement of this ever-existing material a Zion of God can always be built on the earth. (*Discourses of Brigham Young*, 118.)

We are to build up and establish Zion, gather the House of Israel, and redeem the nations of the earth. This people have this work to do, whether we live to see it or not. This is all in our hands. (*Discourses of Brigham Young,* 437.)

We have been commanded to gather ourselves together, to come out of Babylon, and sanctify ourselves, and build up the Zion of our God, by building cities and temples, redeeming countries from the solitude of nature, until the earth is sanctified and prepared for the residence of God and angels. (*Discourses of Brigham Young*, 407.)

Let us train our minds until we delight in that which is good, lovely and holy, seeking continually after that intelligence which will enable us effectually to build up Zion, which consists in building houses, tabernacles, temples, streets, and every convenience and necessity to embellish and beautify, seeking to do the will of the Lord all the days of our lives, improving our minds in all scientific and mechanical knowledge, seeking diligently to understand the great design and plan of all created things, that we may know what to do with our lives and how to improve upon the facilities placed within our reach. (*Discourses of Brigham Young*, 247.)

My heart has been set in me to do the will of God, to build up his Kingdom on the earth, to establish Zion and its laws, and to save the people; and I can say, truly and honestly, that the thought never came into my mind, in all my labors, what my reward will be, or whether my crown would be large or small, or any crown at all, a small possession, a large possession, or no possession. I have never had any thoughts or reflections upon this, or cared the first thing about it. All that I have had in my mind has been that it was my duty to do the will of God, and to labor to establish his Kingdom on the earth because the principles which God has revealed for the salvation of the inhabitants of the earth are pure, holy and exalting in their nature. In them there is honor and eternal increase, they lead on from light to light, strength to strength, glory to glory, knowledge to knowledge, and power to power. (*Discourses of Brigham Young*, 452.)

www.ingramcontent.com/pod-product-compliance
Lightning Source LLC
Chambersburg PA
CBHW071625040426
42452CB00009B/1487